Editorial Project Manager
Eric Migliaccio

Editor in Chief
Karen J. Goldfluss, M.S. Ed.

Creative Director
Sarah M. Fournier

Cover Artist
Sarah Kim

Illustrator
Clint McKnight

Art Coordinator
Renée Mc Elwee

Imaging
Amanda R. Harter

Publisher
Mary D. Smith, M.S. Ed.

Author

Karen McRae

For correlations to the Common Core State Standards, see pages 142–144 of this book or visit *http://www.teachercreated.com/standards/*.

Teacher Created Resources
12621 Western Avenue
Garden Grove, CA 92841
www.teachercreated.com
ISBN: 978-1-4206-2973-6
© 2016 Teacher Created Resources
Made in U.S.A.

TABLE OF CONTENTS

TABLE OF CONTENTS (CONT.)

TABLE OF CONTENTS (CONT.)

+ +

INTRODUCTION

Read through the latest state standards, and you will find that the work expected of students is expressed using such academic terminology as *describe*, *determine*, *develop*, *support*, and *cite*. Requirements such as these cannot be met via the comprehension-question worksheets and culminating quizzes that have long been the staples of literature guides designed for classroom use. The primary objective of those traditional activities was to make sure that students were keeping track of what was happening in the section of the novel that they had just read. Very little rigor and synthesis was asked of students—and usually none until the entire novel was read.

From a teacher's standpoint, this style of classroom analysis misses multiple opportunities to delve deeply into the details that make a specific piece of literature a classic; from a student's standpoint, this way to reflect on literature is monotonous and inflexible, and it fails to nurture the momentum experienced when one is invested in a compelling work of art. That is why the in-depth guides in the *Rigorous Reading* series aim to do much more: they aim to transform the reading of a great novel into a journey of discovery for students.

Instead of merely asking students what happened in any given section, this resource asks questions that require closer reading and deeper analysis—questions such as "Why did the author choose to include this information?" and "How does this information further the plot or offer more insight into the themes, characters, settings, etc.?" And instead of waiting until the end of the novel to put the pieces of the puzzle in place, students will learn to add to and alter their understanding of the novel *as they are reading it*. The various activities in this resource prompt students to consider and appreciate the many ingredients the author has combined to form the novel as a whole.

A RIGOROUS APPROACH

A Customizable Resource

This guide offers you incredible flexibility as you share and explore great literature with your students. The activities contained within are general enough to be used with just about any novel, yet they are designed to be completely customizable to the novel you are teaching. Classic literary works feature certain elements, such as characterization, plot, setting, and theme. By directing attention to these literary elements and the author's reasons for employing them, you will make your students better readers *and* writers.

Teacher Tip #1: Mentor Texts

Use great novels to model great writing. The activities in this resource will get your students thinking about the components of compelling literature. When possible, provide your students with opportunities to try out these literary techniques in their own writing.

Getting Started

The goal of this approach is to systematically build understanding of the novel and of the choices the author made in creating it. In order to do that, the novel should be read and examined section by section.

Teacher Tip #2: Sectioning the Novel

Making each section the same size is not always the best choice. It's more important to consider the ebb, flow, and momentum your young readers experience as they journey through the book. Pay attention to where the natural breaks in action come. Often there are minor resolutions to storylines along the way, and these can be ideal places to stop and reflect on what has happened in the plot and to the characters. Conversely, a chapter may end with a particularly exciting cliffhanger that leaves the reader excited and eager to learn more. Stop there, and look closely at such elements as the following:

- **characterization** (What does this cliffhanger mean for the protagonist?)
- **craft** (Which devices does the author use to build up to this moment and create this effect?)
- **plot** (Based on the context of the story, what will likely happen next? What are the possible consequences of what could happen next?)

Once you have decided on how to divide the novel, have students begin to read the first section. You may also wish to distribute some pre-reading activities.

Teacher Tip #3: Limited Frontloading

With this more rigorous approach to analyzing literature, less frontloading of the material is required. Almost all student work should focus on the text. However, this guide does offer a select few pre-reading activity ideas on pages 10–14.

A RIGOROUS APPROACH (CONT.)

Getting Started (cont.)

Before distributing activities for the first section of the novel, have each student assemble his or her own Interactive Novel Log.

> **Teacher Tip #4: Interactive Novel Logs**
>
> These student-created resources give the individual members of your class a place and a space to connect with the novel in ways of their choosing. For more information on what to include in these Interactive Novel Logs and how to create them, see pages 8-9 in this guide.

Studying Each Section of the Novel

After students have completed their reading of a section of the novel, distribute copies of the activities that best fit the content of that section. Each section begins with a "Teacher Instructions" page that provides an overview of each activity in that section.

This guide is organized by the literary elements found in great literature.

- **Characterization & P.O.V.** (pages 15–34)
  Analyze character traits, development, and growth. Examine relationships between characters. Consider narrative perspective and how it affects the story.

- **Plot & Structure** (pages 35–57)
  Summarize and sequence events. Examine the types of conflict in the story. Analyze the structure and organization of the novel and the parts within it.

> **Teacher Tip #5: Learning Types**
>
> Most activities are labeled as either **Individual** or **Collaborative** on the "Teacher Instructions" pages. The majority of the activities, however, can be adapted to fit any type of learning environment.

- **Setting & Genre** (pages 58–70)
  List physical settings, noting how the author describes them and how they contribute to the tone and plot of the story. Pay attention to the author's use of time period and the passage of time. Analyze genre elements.

- **Main Idea & Theme** (pages 71–79)
  Look at the big ideas and the themes that are woven throughout the story.
  (If help is needed determining the themes of the specific novel being taught, using the online search term "Themes for [name of novel]" should provide a few websites that offer helpful information.)

- **Author's Craft** (pages 80–100)
  Pay close attention to such authorial choices as pacing, chapter length, and how chapters begin and end. Examine the use of imagery and how the author establishes mood and reveals tone. Search for examples of literary devices and note the effects they create.

- **Vocabulary** (pages 101–105)
  Examine word choice. Identify unknown words and use context to determine meaning.

A RIGOROUS APPROACH (CONT.)

After Finishing the Novel

As the story is being read, many of the activities described previously can be used to build layers of understanding of both the story as a whole and the elements that have been combined to create it. A lot of synthesis is included in those activities on pages 15–105 of this guide.

The following activities call for even more synthesis and include larger projects and essays to culminate your class's exploration of the novel.

◆ **Post-Reading Activities** (pages 106–126)
Plan, draft, write, and review essays. Create a class encyclopedia devoted to the novel. Choose from several group projects that appeal to multiple learning styles.

Using Paired Texts in the Classroom

The use of multiple texts can help build and extend knowledge about a theme or topic. It can also illustrate the similarities and differences in how multiple authors approach similar content or how an individual author approaches multiple novels. This guide offers several activities designed to be used with text sets. These activities can be used when pairing any two works of fiction, be they novels or shorter story forms.

◆ **Text-Set Connections** (pages 127–139)
Examine and compare the characterization of the protagonists, antagonists, and supporting characters in two works of fiction. Compare and contrast each author's use of perspective, setting, conflict, theme, and other literary elements.

Bonus Resources

Additionally, this guide contains two useful bonus handouts. A glossary of literary terms (page 140) gives students a quick explanation of many of the terms discussed in this guide. Similarly, a list of fiction genres (page 141) is provided to give students an overview and explanation of the most common genres they will encounter in works of fiction.

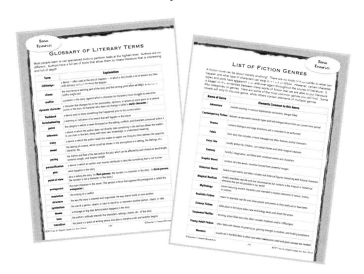

Meeting Standards

A complete list of the Common Core State Standards met by the activities in this guide can be found on pages 142–144. (**Note:** The standards correlations provided on these pages focus on the grades 6–8 range. However, teacher discretion should be used to determine if any activity is appropriate for lower or higher grades, as well.)

KEEPING NOVEL LOGS

Overview

Great works of literature are complex texts, and complex texts are multilayered. They enrich and reveal as they go along. Successful readers are those who "go along" with the novel, too. Interactive Novel Logs give students a place and a space to record their thoughts and observations as they journey through the book.

How It Works

After each section of the novel is read, students use their Interactive Novel Logs to track the introduction and development of such literary elements as plot, setting, theme, characterization, craft, and structure. Do this by distributing new copies of the following activity pages:

- ◆ "A Dynamic Protagonist" (page 18)
- ◆ "Major Minors" (page 19)
- ◆ "The Summaries of Its Parts" (page 38)
- ◆ "A Quartet of Conflicts" (page 42)
- ◆ "I Predict" (page 52)
- ◆ "Location, Location" (page 60)
- ◆ "What's the Big Idea?" (page 73)
- ◆ "Checking In on Theme" (page 75)

- ◆ "The Long and Short of It" (page 83)
- ◆ "Beginnings and Endings" (page 85)
- ◆ "Making the Mood" (page 91)
- ◆ "Left in Suspense" (page 96)
- ◆ "My Word Wall" (page 102)
- ◆ "Choice Words" (page 103)
- ◆ "Alike and Opposite" (page 104)

In addition to repeating and completing these activities throughout the course of reading the novel, students should also be encouraged to connect the novel to their own lives. Located at the end of most sections, the "Log-In" pages provide a perfect way to do this. These pages give students several ideas and options to further explore the text and apply aspects of its contents to their own experiences. By offering multiple suggestions, these "Ideas for Your Interactive Novel Log" can appeal to all types of learners. And while the prompts encourage personal response, they are still connected to the themes and ideas presented in the novel.

Teacher Tip #6: Preview the Prompts

Consider allowing your students to preview the "Ideas for Your Interactive Novel Log" prompts a day or two before they are asked to respond to them. This type of writing requires rumination. When asking students to reflect on past experiences and articulate their personal connections to a work of art, give them the time and space needed for their thoughts to percolate to the surface. By allowing your students to sit with the ideas presented in these prompts, you will relieve the pressure an immediate response can cause.

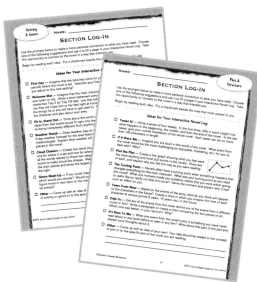

KEEPING NOVEL LOGS (CONT.)

How It Works (cont.)

Here is a list of the "Log-In" pages and where they can be found:

- ◆ for the Characterization & P.O.V. section (page 34)
- ◆ for the Plot & Structure section (page 57)
- ◆ for the Setting & Genre section (page 70)
- ◆ for the Main Idea & Theme section (page 79)
- ◆ for the Author's Craft section (page 100)
- ◆ for the Text-Set Connections section (page 139)

Assembling the Interactive Novel Logs

Use the following instructions to assemble an Interactive Novel Log for each of your students.

Materials needed for each student:

- a ½-inch three-ring binder or presentation folder
- a blank, hole-punched sheet of plain paper for title page
- two or three sheets of lined paper for Table of Contents
- several extra sheets of paper (both lined and plain) for student's responses to the "Ideas for Your Interactive Novel Log" prompts at the end of each section.

Directions:

1. On the plain paper, allow students to design their own title page. Have them write "Interactive Novel Log" and the title of the novel in the middle of the page. They should include their name and grade at the bottom. Allow students to decorate the page.

2. Add blank lined paper for the Table of Contents. Have students write "Table of Contents" at the top. They will add to this list as they create new pages.

3. Before reading each section of the novel, photocopy and distribute new copies of the Interactive Novel Log worksheets (see page 8 for a complete list).

4. For the final activity in each section, photocopy and distribute the "Log-In" page for the section. Follow the directions given. Students select one or more of the topics in the "Ideas for Your Interactive Novel Log" section and create an Interactive Novel Log page that responds to that topic.

5. After the class has completed the entire novel and the post-reading activities, you may wish to have students include the "My Book Rating" worksheet (page 126) as a final entry in their Interactive Novel Logs.

TEACHER INSTRUCTIONS

Before your students begin reading the novel, use the following worksheets to prepare them for the experience of reading and analyzing a work of literature.

Note: With this more rigorous approach to analyzing literature, less frontloading of the material is required. Almost all student work should initially focus on the text, not on students' personal experiences. For this reason, this section is considerably shorter than subsequent sections. Once students have read and studied parts of the novel, they can then use their understanding of the text to make personal connections through the use of Interactive Novel Logs.

+ +

Activity: "The Reader"   **Page #:** 11   **Learning Type:** Collaborative
Description: Begin the reading process by analyzing yourself as a reader. What types of characters, events, and genres are you drawn to? What types do you tend to dislike? Strengthen speaking skills by explaining your preferences to a partner. Exhibit listening skills by summarizing your partner's preferences. Together, discuss the role of the reader in how a novel is experienced.

Activity: "Quick Takes on Topics"   **Page #:** 12   **Learning Type:** Individual
Description: Think deeply about some of the topics that the novel will explore. Prior to reading the novel, record thoughts and opinions about those topics. Examine what ideas you, the reader, are bringing with you as you begin the process of reading the novel.
Teacher Tip: Choose four topics, ideas, themes, etc., that are prominently featured in the novel. Have students write each of these four on the appropriate lines on the worksheet. Here are some examples of topics/themes for specific novels:

  ✦ *Holes* — camps, crime, class, curses, group interaction, fate

  ✦ *Charlotte's Web* — friendship, growing up, the cycle of life, sacrifice, the power of language

  ✦ *Wonder* – being different, bullying, choosing kindness, considering other people's perspective(s), taking responsibility for your actions

Activity: "Judging a Book"   **Page #:** 13   **Learning Type:** Individual
Description: Take a few minutes to think about the title of the novel, as well as the cover. Record thoughts about what each of these elements might suggest about the content you are about to read.

Activity: "The Writer"   **Page #:** 14   **Learning Type:** Individual
Description: Do research to learn more about the author of the novel you are about to read. In your own words, write a short biography of this author. Detail the successes he or she has achieved, along with the challenges he or she has faced.
Teacher Tip: Stress to students the necessity for using their own words in any research-based writing project. Talk to them about plagiarism and explain that specific wording taken directly from a source must be written within quotation marks.

Here's Another Idea: Heroes and Villains

Many novels feature heroes and villains. Ask your students to share their thoughts on these two classic character types. Have them list traits that define each type. Ask them to offer and explain examples of heroes and villains from other novels, as well as from films, television shows, and other works of art. Ask them if they think a novel needs heroes and/or villains to be interesting.

THE READER

You are about to read a novel. That means that you are about to become the reader. What kind of reader are you?

Work with a partner. For each category below, tell your partner the things you seem to like or dislike in what you read. Listen to your partner's answers, too.

Characters (the people and/or creatures in the story)

Questions: What types of characters do you tend to like reading about? Why?

What types of characters do you tend to dislike reading about? Why?

Plot (the events that happen in the story)

Questions: What types of events do you tend to like reading about? Why?

What types of events do you tend to dislike reading about? Why?

Genre (the type of story — for example, science fiction, adventure, realistic fiction)

Questions: What types of stories do you tend to like reading? Why?

What types of stories do you tend to dislike reading? Why?

✦ ✦

On the lines below, summarize your partner's responses. Briefly tell which kinds of characters, events, and genres your partner likes to read about and what types he/she does not usually like to read about.

_____

_____

_____

_____

_____

_____

Work together again to answer this one final question: *Is the reader an important part of any novel? Why or why not?* Come up with an answer and write it on the lines below.

_____

_____

_____

_____

NAME: _____

QUICK TAKES ON TOPICS

Each reader begins a book with his or her own ideas, opinions, and tidbits of knowledge. The book you are about to read explores many ideas and topics. Your teacher will give you four such topics that will be featured in the novel you are about to read. For each, write a little about the thoughts and opinions you are bringing with you as you begin the journey of reading this novel.

+ +

Idea or Topic #1 _____

What does this mean to you or make you think of? _____

_____

_____

_____

Idea or Topic #2 _____

What does this mean to you or make you think of? _____

_____

_____

_____

Idea or Topic #3 _____

What does this mean to you or make you think of? _____

_____

_____

_____

Idea or Topic #4 _____

What does this mean to you or make you think of? _____

_____

_____

_____

NAME: _____

JUDGING A BOOK

You are about to read a novel. Before you even open the book, answer these questions.

1. What is the title of the novel, and who wrote it? _____

_____

2. Think about the title of the book. Based on the title, what do you expect the mood of the novel to be? Place a checkmark next to any or all of the following:

☐ adventurous ☐ funny ☐ heartwarming ☐ sad

☐ scary ☐ silly ☐ heartbreaking ☐ tense

Explain your choice(s) here.

_____

_____

_____

Now pick up the book. You have probably heard the saying, "Don't judge a book by its cover," but let's do it anyway.

3. Briefly describe the colors on the front of the book.

_____

_____

4. Briefly describe the images on the front of the book.

_____

_____

5. Briefly describe the style(s) and size(s) in which the letters in the title are printed.

_____

_____

6. In a few sentences, describe the mood evoked by the colors, images, and letter styles on the front of the book. In other words, based on these elements, what impressions and feelings do you have about the book you are about to read?

_____

_____

_____

_____

NAME: _____

THE WRITER

The book you are about to read is mostly here because of the ideas and efforts of one person: the author. Learn more about this person.

Use online or print sources (encyclopedias, etc.) to research information about the person who wrote the novel. In your own words, write a brief biography of this writer. Try to include as many of the following details as possible:

| where and when the author was born | how and when the author began writing career | challenges the author has faced | titles of some of the author's best-known books | major awards the author has won |

_____
_____
_____
_____
_____
_____
_____
_____
_____
_____
_____
_____
_____
_____
_____
_____
_____
_____
_____
_____
_____
_____

TEACHER INSTRUCTIONS

The term **characterization** refers to how the author creates and describes the appearance, thoughts, actions, and reactions of the people who populate the world of the novel. **Point of view** refers to the perspective of the narrator who is presenting the novel to the reader.

Distribute "A Quick Guide to . . ." (page 17), which gives an overview and examples of characterization and point of view, along with an in-depth look at a key term. You may also have students consult the "Glossary of Literary Terms" resource (page 140) to check understanding of literary terms related to characterization and point of view.

+ +

As your students read the novel, use the following worksheets to help them analyze and examine aspects related to characterization and point of view.

    Activities marked with this icon are meant to be used after the reading of each section of the novel. At that time, distribute fresh copies of these pages. Completed copies should be included in each student's Interactive Novel Log.

Activity: "A Dynamic Protagonist"   **Page #:** 18   **Learning Type:** Individual
Description: Describe the protagonist at both the beginning and end of the section. Track growth and identify the causes of change.

Activity: "Major Minors"   **Page #:** 19   **Learning Type:** Individual
Description: Examine the minor characters involved in each section of the novel. Determine what they add to our understanding of the main character or to the novel as a whole.

Activity: "Getting to Know a Character"   **Page #:** 20   **Learning Type:** Collaborative
Description: Work with a partner to examine the way a character is viewed by himself/herself and by others. Provide textual evidence for all claims.
Teacher Tip: This worksheet is ideally suited for analyzing the novel's protagonist, but it can also be used to examine other characters.

Activity: "Character Study"   **Page #:** 21   **Learning Type:** Individual
Description: Take an inventory of the protagonist's "possessions" (e.g., personality traits, support system). Also think about what makes the character feel comfortable or safe and which events in the novel endanger this feeling.

Activity: "Highs and Lows"   **Page #:** 22   **Learning Type:** Collaborative
Description: Practice speaking, listening, and paraphrasing skills while listing the high and low points of the protagonist's journey. Discuss how and when these events happen in the novel, as well as the effect these events have on the reader.

Activity: "Who Had What Effect?"   **Page #:** 23   **Learning Type:** Individual
Description: Decide which secondary character most influenced the protagonist and which one was the most supportive. Support claims with evidence. Compare characters.

NAME: _____

TEACHER INSTRUCTIONS (CONT.)

Activity: "Mirror, Mirror" **Page #:** 24 **Learning Type:** Individual
Description: Compare and contrast characters who are most similar to and most different from the protagonist in specific ways.

Activity: "Those Who Oppose" **Page #:** 25 **Learning Type:** Individual
Description: Catalog the behaviors and motivations of the antagonist(s) in the novel. Determine why the author chose to include either multiple antagonists or just one.

Activity: "All Together Now" **Page #:** 26 **Learning Type:** Collaborative
Description: Working in groups, locate a scene in the novel that exemplifies the personalities of multiple characters. Show how this one scene displays certain traits of each character's personality in certain situations.
Teacher Tip: Divide the class into groups of three or four. Within each group, have each student focus on a different character from a chosen scene.

Activity: "Acting One's Age" **Page #:** 27 **Learning Type:** Individual
Description: Sort the novel's characters by age, and then look for commonality within those groups. Find and support examples of characters acting more or less mature than their ages would suggest. Consider the importance of the adult characters in the novel.

Activity: "Says Who?" **Page #:** 28 **Learning Type:** Individual
Description: Determine the point of view of the novel's narrator and reflect on how well the reader comes to "know" the narrator.

Activity: "Says You" **Page #:** 29 **Learning Type:** Collaborative
Description: Building on the previous activity, work with partners to discuss how the novel would change if the point of view of its narrator changed.

Activity: "A New Perspective" **Page #:** 30 **Learning Type:** Individual/Collaborative
Description: Rewrite a scene from an alternate point of view. As an extension activity, exchange papers and discuss how this new perspective affects the way the scene reads.

Activity: "More Than One" **Page #:** 31 **Learning Type:** Individual
Description: Examine the author's use of multiple narrators. Determine why this choice was made and how it served the material well.
Teacher Tip: This activity is designed to be used only with novels that feature multiple narrators, such as the following: *Wonder, The View from Saturday, Counting by 7s*.

Activity: "The Lead Singer" **Page #:** 32 **Learning Type:** Individual
Description: Analyze the novel's narrative voice and consider why the author would choose this style of voice to describe the events of this particular novel.

Activity: "Comparing Voices" **Page #:** 33 **Learning Type:** Individual
Description: Cite evidence to show how the author gave distinct voices to three characters from the novel.

Activity: "Section Log-In" **Page #:** 34 **Learning Type:** Individual
Description: Choose from several options to add to Interactive Novel Logs.

A QUICK GUIDE TO . . .

Characterization → the appearance, personality, and actions of each character in a novel

Point of View (P.O.V.) → the identity and perspective of the narrator

Elements in Action → from *Wonder* by R.J. Palacio

Characterization	Point of View (P.O.V.)
The protagonist, Auggie, narrates part of the book. This gives readers a direct line to his thoughts and feelings. Through the narration and reactions of other characters, we also view Auggie through other people's eyes. The novel's one detailed description of Auggie's physical appearance is narrated by Via, Auggie's loving, supportive, protective older sister.	In all, this novel features six narrators. This use of multiple narrators serves both functional and thematic purposes. It gives readers access to the thoughts of multiple characters, and it reminds us that each person's experiences inform his/her viewpoints and are the basis for his/her actions and reactions.

Spotlight On → **First-Person vs. Third-Person**

Related Ideas: voice, perspective, limited, omniscient

The author's choice of a specific point of view for a novel relates to his or her purpose. The author may want readers to feel a deeper connection with one character and hear the story from just that character's perspective. Or, the author may want to use a narrator who is completely separate from the story and who can give the reader a more thorough understanding of all of the characters and events in the novel. For authors, this choice begins with the decision to write in first-person or third-person.

P.O.V.	Explanation	Limited or Omniscient?
First-Person	A character in the story is the narrator who describes what he or she sees, hears, feels, and thinks. The character uses such pronouns as *I*, *my*, or *we* to describe himself/herself.	Almost always **limited**. A first-person narrator can tell the reader only as much as his or her character knows. The only exceptions would be if an all-knowing god or a character with this supernatural power were the narrator.
Third-Person	The narrator is not a character in the story. This type of narrator does not use words such as *I*, *my*, or *we* to describe himself/herself.	Either. An **omniscient** third-person narrator is able to tell the reader what *any* character is doing, feeling, thinking, or saying. A **limited** third-person narrator can only tell the reader what *one* character is feeling or thinking or what actions occur when that one character is there.

NAME: _____

A DYNAMIC PROTAGONIST

Characters in novels can either be static or dynamic. A **static character** stays the same throughout the novel. The characteristics that define that character remain the same. A **dynamic character** does not stay the same. He or she grows and changes in some way or in many ways.

The **protagonist** is the main character or central figure in a novel. Often, the novel is about the attitudes, actions, and experiences of the protagonist.

As you read each section of the novel, examine the protagonist's growth as a character.

+ +

Chapters or page numbers in section: _____

+ +

1. Who is the protagonist of this section of the novel? _____

2. Complete the following chart. Choose two traits that describe this protagonist at the beginning and end of this section of the novel. Support your choices.

	Trait #1	**Trait #2**
at the **beginning** of this section	*Trait:* *Example:*	*Trait:* *Example:*
at the **end** of this section	*Trait:* *Example:*	*Trait:* *Example:*

3. Do the protagonist's thoughts, actions, or feelings change much during this section of the novel? Explain your answer.

_____

_____

_____

Give reasons from the text for why the protagonist changed in these ways.

_____

_____

_____

MAJOR MINORS

It is common for a novel to have one major character and for the novel's plot to revolve around this character. However, most novels also have many minor characters. They are important, too.

Fill out the chart below with information about each minor character. Only include information from the section you have just read. Think about the following:

✦ Does this section give you any ideas about why the author included this character in the book?

✦ In this section, how does the character add to the themes of the novel or give us more insight into the main character?

+ +

Chapters or page numbers in section: _____

+ +

Character's Name	Information and Ideas

NAME(S): _____

GETTING TO KNOW A CHARACTER

Look closely at how an author helps us get to know a character. Work with a partner to complete this worksheet. Find quotations from the book to support your claims.

+ +

Getting to Know _____ from _____
(name of character)   (name of novel)

1. How does this character act when he or she is alone? _____

_____

   Example: _____

_____ Page number(s): _____

2. How does this character act when he or she is with other people? _____

_____

   Example: _____

_____ Page number(s): _____

3. How do this character's friends and/or family describe him or her? _____

_____

   Example: _____

_____ Page number(s): _____

4. How do other people treat this character? _____

_____

   Example: _____

_____ Page number(s): _____

5. How does this character describe himself/herself? _____

_____

   Example: _____

_____ Page number(s): _____

6. How would you describe this character to someone who hasn't read the book?

_____

_____

NAME: _____

CHARACTER STUDY

Taking Inventory

When you take inventory, you see <u>what you have</u> and <u>how much of it you have</u>. Complete the diagram below to show what this character possesses, or has.

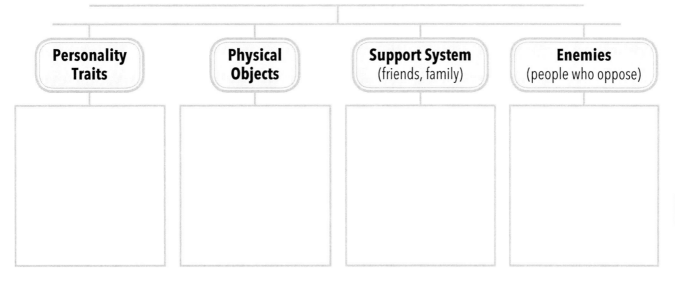

Name of Character:

| **Personality Traits** | **Physical Objects** | **Support System** (friends, family) | **Enemies** (people who oppose) |

Comfort Zone

Think about what the character likes to do and where he or she likes to be.

1. In what kinds of situations does the character feel comfortable or safe?

_____

_____

Quotation that shows this: _____

_____

_____ Page number(s): _____

2. What events in the novel force the character out of his/her comfort zone?

_____

_____

_____

How do these events do this? _____

_____

_____

NAME(S): _____

HIGHS AND LOWS

Work with a partner to name two highs and two lows the main character experiences during the novel. Alternate roles.

✦ Each answer should be given aloud by the speaker.

✦ The listener should use his/her own words to record the speaker's answer.

Speaker's Name: _____ Listener's Name: _____

	What Event Happens?	**What Caused the Event?**	**How Does the Character React?**
High Point (Positive)			
Low Point (Negative)			

Speaker's Name: _____ Listener's Name: _____

	What Event Happens?	**What Caused the Event?**	**How Does the Character React?**
High Point (Positive)			
Low Point (Negative)			

✦ ✦

Discuss with your partner: What effects on the reader do the high points have? Why? What effects on the reader do the low points have? Why? On a separate piece of paper, summarize your discussion.

NAME: _____

WHO HAD WHAT EFFECT?

Think about the secondary or supporting characters in the novel. What effect did they have on the protagonist? Which one most influenced the main character? Which one was the most supportive to the main character?

✦ To **influence** means to somehow lead, encourage, or cause someone to do something — positive or negative — that he or she might not normally have done.

✦ To **support** means to give someone the help they need to accomplish something.

✦ ✦

1. The protagonist was most **influenced** by _____ because

_____

_____

_____.

Quotation or example: _____

_____

_____ Page number(s): _____

2. The protagonist was most **supported** by _____ because

_____

_____

_____.

Quotation or example: _____

_____

_____ Page number(s): _____

3. Are the two characters you named more similar or different from one another? Explain.

_____

_____

_____

_____

_____

_____

NAME: _____

MIRROR, MIRROR

Think of the image that looks back at you when you look in a mirror. It looks just like you, but it is also your exact opposite. Complete the thoughts below to show who is most alike and most unalike the protagonist of the novel.

1. Who possesses a trait that is most similar to that of the main character?

_____ and _____ are both _____
(protagonist)   (other character)   (trait they have in common)

because they _____

_____.

Provide evidence to support your point. Summarize a scene or use a quotation that shows this trait in each character.

Protagonist's scene or quotation: _____

_____

_____ Page number(s): _____

Other character's scene or quotation: _____

_____

_____ Page number(s): _____

2. Who possesses a trait that is the exact opposite of the main character?

_____ is _____ while _____
(protagonist)   (trait)   (other character)

is _____. As a result of this, _____
    (trait)

_____

_____.

Provide evidence to support your point. Summarize a scene or use a quotation that shows these opposing traits in each character.

Protagonist's scene or quotation: _____

_____

_____ Page number(s): _____

Other character's scene or quotation: _____

_____

_____ Page number(s): _____

THOSE WHO OPPOSE

In literature, the person or force that opposes (goes against) the **protagonist** (main character) of the story is called the **antagonist**. This word has the same origin as the word **antagonize**, which means "to cause to struggle against."

In a novel, there can be one antagonist or many. If there are many, they can be completely separate from one another, or some or all of them can belong to one group.

_____ contains **one   a few   many**   antagonist(s).
(title of novel)   *(circle one)*

Find four examples of a character or force that opposes the main character. If possible, explain why this person/force is antagonizing the protagonist in this chapter or scene.

Chapter or Scene	Name(s) of Antagonist(s)	Behavior Toward Protagonist	Motivation for Behavior

+ +

Considering Craft: The author of this novel chose to have either just one antagonist or to have multiple (more than one) antagonists. Why do you think the author made the choice he/she made? How does having that number of "bad guys" best serve the novel? Use examples from the text to support your answer.

_____

_____

_____

_____

_____

NAME(S): _____

ALL TOGETHER NOW

For this activity, work in small groups. As a group, locate a passage or scene in the novel that includes several characters — at least one character for each member in your group. Try to find a scene in which each character's personality is on display. In other words, the dialogue or action in the scene should show at least one trait of each character in the scene.

Begin by brainstorming ideas for possible scenes that would work well for this activity.

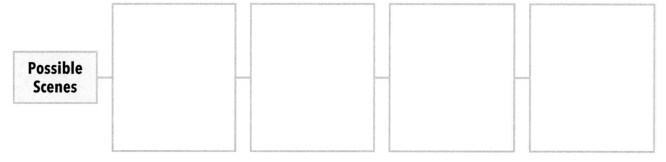

Possible Scenes

Then make a final decision:

The scene our group chose is _____.

Have each member of your group represent at least one character in the scene. On a separate piece of paper, answer the following questions about "your" character.

1. How does the character act in this scene?

2. What types of things does the character say in this scene? Provide a quotation from the scene.

3. How is the character's behavior in this scene a good example of how that character acts throughout the novel?

4. Does this character act differently when he/she is in a group of people than when he/she is alone or with just one other character? If so, what about this group influences this character to act in this way?

When you are finished analyzing your character's behavior, meet again as a group. Discuss each character's behavior. Then, as a group, answer the following question. Summarize your group's answer on the lines below.

5. How does this one scene illustrate how the group acts throughout the whole novel?

_____

_____

_____

_____

_____

ACTING ONE'S AGE

Novels written for children or young adults usually feature important characters who are children or young adults themselves. Adult characters usually play secondary roles in these types of novels. Use this worksheet to look at the behaviors of characters of all ages in the novel.

1. Who are the younger characters in the novel? Who are the older ones?

Children/Teenagers	Adults

2. If possible, name one thing besides age that the younger characters seem to have in common. Provide an example from the novel.

_____

_____

3. If possible, name one thing besides age that the older characters seem to have in common. Provide an example from the novel.

_____

_____

4. Name one character who — at some point in the novel — acts younger than his/her chronological (time) age. Support your answer with an example from the text.

_____

_____

5. Name one character who — at some point in the novel — acts older than his/her chronological (time) age. Support your answer with an example from the text.

_____

_____

6. In your opinion, which adult character is the most important to the plot of the novel? Use textual evidence to support your answer.

_____

_____

NAME: _____

SAYS WHO?

All novels have a **narrator**, a person (or other being) who recounts the events of the novel.

✦ Sometimes the narrator is an actual character in the novel. This type is called a **first-person** narrator. He or she uses pronouns such as *I*, *me*, *we*, and *us* to describe his or her role in the events of the novel.

✦ Sometimes the narrator is *not* a character in the novel. This type is called a **third-person** narrator. He or she uses pronouns such as *he*, *her*, and *them* to describe the roles of all of the characters in the novel.

✦ A third-person narrator can be **omniscient** (able to hear the thoughts and see the actions of all characters) or **limited** (only able to tell about events that happen when a specific character is present).

+ +

Name of Novel: _____

1. Is the narrator a character in the novel? *(circle one)*   **Yes**   **No**

Explain how or why you know this. _____

_____

2. Based on your answer to #1, the novel has a   **first-person   third-person**   narrator.
⌐*(circle one)*⌐

Depending on your answer to #2, complete one of the following columns of questions:

First-Person Narrator	Third-Person Narrator
3. Is the narrator also the novel's main character? If not, explain who the narrator is. _____ _____	*3.* Can the narrator tell you the thoughts inside all of the characters' heads? Explain. _____ _____
4. How well do you feel you get to know the personality of this narrator? Explain why you feel this way. _____ _____ _____ _____	*4.* How well do you feel you get to know the personality of this narrator? Explain why you feel this way. _____ _____ _____ _____

28

SAYS YOU

Work with a partner as you follow the instructions given below. Use your answers from the "Says Who?" worksheet as a basis for this activity. Together, fill in the blanks to complete this paragraph:

Today, we are discussing a novel called _____.

This novel has a _____-person narrator.

Then decide who will be Speaker #1 and who will be Speaker #2.

+ +

Speaker #1: _____   **Speaker #2:** _____

First	Speaker #1 should answer the following question aloud to his/her partner: *How would the novel have changed if the author had written the story from a different point of view?* Speaker #1 should give two specific examples of how the novel would be different.
Next	Speaker #2 should listen to Speaker #1's answer and paraphrase it on the lines below. He or she should then think of another example of how the novel would be different, and he or she should say this example aloud to Speaker #1.

_____

_____

_____

_____

Then	Speaker #2 should answer the following question aloud to his/her partner: *Why do you think the author chose to use the type of narrator that he or she used in this novel?* Speaker #2 should give two specific reasons.
Lastly	Speaker #1 should listen to Speaker #2's answer and paraphrase it on the lines below. He or she should then think of another reason for why the author chose this type of narrator, and he or she should say this reason aloud to Speaker #1.

_____

_____

_____

_____

_____

NAME: _____

A NEW PERSPECTIVE

Choose an important, interesting, or entertaining scene from the novel. How does the author's choice of narrator affect this scene? How would the scene read differently if it were told by a different type of narrator?

Which scene did you choose?	

Rewrite the scene. Use a different type of narrator.

_____

_____

_____

_____

_____

_____

_____

_____

_____

_____

_____

_____

_____

_____

_____

_____

_____

_____

+ +

Discuss with a partner: Once you are done, exchange papers with a partner. Have him or her identify the new type of narrator (first-person or third-person, limited or omniscient). Discuss how a new type of narrator would change the scene for the reader.

NAME: _____

MORE THAN ONE

Most novels have just one narrator, but there some that have more. Some novels switch from one first-person narrator to another (and maybe even more than that). Other novels switch from a first-person narrator to a third-person narrator, or vice versa. Either way, the use of multiple narrators is unusual, and so you know the author is doing it for a reason.

1. List all of the narrators in this novel. Also, describe the scenes — or types of scenes — they narrate.

Narrator	Scenes Narrated

2. Can you distinguish any pattern as to why a certain narrator would narrate one scene while a different narrator would narrate another? Explain.

_____

_____

_____

_____

3. What is the result of this choice the author made to have more than one narrator? How did this choice change or add to the novel? Give your thoughts here, along with examples from the novel.

_____

_____

_____

_____

_____

_____

_____

_____

NAME: _____

THE LEAD SINGER

One very important tool an author can use to establish point of view is **voice**. In writing, the term *voice* can describe the style and/or personality of the way a character speaks or thinks. It can also be used to describe the style and/or personality of the way a narrator describes the characters, settings, and events. Since the narrator's voice can be "heard" on every page, he or she is a bit like the lead singer of the novel.

1. Is the narrator a character in the novel?   **Yes**   **No**

✦ If **Yes**, which character is he or she? _____

✦ If **No**, is the narrator **limited** or **omniscient**? _____

2. Use three words to describe the voice of the narrator. For each, provide a quotation from the novel that supports your word choice.

Descriptive Word	Quotation from Novel

3. What do you think the author's purpose was for choosing a narrator like this? How does this type of narrator fit the content, mood, or style of the book?

_____

_____

_____

4. Rewrite the first line of the novel (or the first line of any chapter). Use a very different narrative voice.

_____

_____

_____

If the entire novel had been written in this new voice, in what ways would that have changed it?

_____

_____

_____

COMPARING VOICES

Each character has a voice. In literature, this term does not usually refer to the sound characters' vocal cords make when they speak but to the **style** and **characteristics** of their speech. In other words, it's about the words they use and the way they use them.

Most authors try to make their characters sound unique. They want their individual characters to have different speech patterns, use different words, etc.

Use your experience as a reader to come up with an idea of why most authors try to do this.

_____

_____

+ +

In the novel you are reading, in what ways does the author make his/her characters' voices different? Focus on three characters. Give specific examples from the novel.

Character #1 is named _____.

Here is how I would describe the way this character speaks or thinks: _____

_____

Here is a quotation that really shows this character's voice: _____

_____

Character #2 is named _____.

Here is how I would describe the way this character speaks or thinks: _____

_____

Here is a quotation that really shows this character's voice: _____

_____

Character #3 is named _____.

Here is how I would describe the way this character speaks or thinks: _____

_____

Here is a quotation that really shows this character's voice: _____

_____

+ +

For Further Consideration: Answer these questions on the back of this paper: *Are there any characters who have very similar voices? Who are these characters, and how are they related in the novel? What is the author trying to show you with this choice?*

NAME: _____

SECTION LOG-IN

Use the prompts below to make a more personal connection to what you have read. Choose one of the following suggestions and use it to fill a page in your Interactive Novel Log. Take this opportunity to connect to the novel in a way that interests you.

Begin by reading each idea. Put a checkmark beside the ones that most appeal to you.

+ +

Ideas for Your Interactive Novel Log

☐ **Most and Least Like Me** — Most novels are filled with characters. In this novel, which character is the most like you, and why? Which character is the least like you? Divide a page in half. Devote each half to one of these questions.

☐ **Words of Wisdom** — Often in novels, there is one character who seems the wisest or most thoughtful. Who is that character in this novel? Is there a person like that in your life? Divide a page in half. Devote one half to the character from the novel and the other half to the person you know.

☐ **The Award Goes To . . .** — Design a few different awards or trophies for categories such as "Kindest," "Most Clever," or "Most Likely to Be President." Be creative in coming up with categories. Write short blurbs explaining to which character you would award each trophy and why.

☐ **Three New Views** — Choose three interesting characters, none of whom are the narrator of the novel. Divide your page in thirds. On each third, write one character's name and explain how the book would be different if that character were the narrator. What would be interesting about a book written from that character's perspective? What new events would the reader get to read about? What events from the book would have to be changed or cut out entirely?

☐ **The Good and the Bad** — Write a letter to one of the characters. Give that character an honest review of his/her words and actions. Mention some good things he or she did, and why you feel those things are positive. Also mention some not-so-good things he or she did. Give advice about a better way these situations could have been handled. Be constructive in your criticism.

☐ **Team Captain** — Imagine you are about to play a team game. It can be a sports game, a board game, or any other type of competition. You have been named team captain and are in charge of assigning jobs or positions to all six members of your team. Those six members are characters from the novel. It is your job to decide what each character's strengths are and to give each character an appropriate job that will help your team succeed. Name the game, the job of each character, and why that character is the perfect fit for that particular job.

☐ **Other** — Come up with an idea of your own! Your idea should be related to the concept of characterization or to a specific character/narrator from the novel you are reading.

_____

_____

TEACHER INSTRUCTIONS

The term **plot** refers to what happens in the story. It describes the events and complications (**conflicts**) that move the story along. **Structure** refers to the way that a novel — and all of the parts within it — is ordered and organized.

Distribute "A Quick Guide to . . ." (page 37), which gives an overview and examples of plot and structure, along with an in-depth look at a key term. You may also have students consult the "Glossary of Literary Terms" resource (page 140) to reference related literary terms.

✦ ✦

As your students read the novel, use the following worksheets to help them analyze and examine aspects related to plot and structure.

🔄 *Activities marked with this icon are meant to be used after the reading of each section of the novel. At that time, distribute fresh copies of these pages. Completed copies should be included in each student's Interactive Novel Log.*

Activity: "The Summaries of Its Parts" 🔄   **Page #:** 38   **Learning Type:** Individual
Description: Practice summarization skills by listing the major plot points of the section just read. Choose and describe an interesting idea, character, or line from the section.
Teacher Tip: This worksheet is to be completed after each section of the novel is read. For a plot breakdown of the entire novel, use the "Major Plot Points" activity.

Activity: "Major Plot Points"   **Page #:** 39   **Learning Type:** Individual
Description: Examine the major plot points of the beginning, middle, and end of the novel. Choose three for each section and use textual evidence to support each choice.

Activity: "In the Beginning"   **Page #:** 40   **Learning Type:** Individual
Description: Examine the novel's opening scene. Decide the style and mood it establishes. Determine if there are clues that signal a change in either style or mood.

Activity: "Getting to Know a Novel"   **Page #:** 41   **Learning Type:** Collaborative
Description: Examine the first few pages of the novel to determine the background information the author supplies about characters, settings, and situations.

Activity: "A Quartet of Conflicts" 🔄   **Page #:** 42   **Learning Type:** Individual
Description: Learn about four common types of conflict and provide examples of each from the section of the novel just read. Locate quotations that illustrate each example.

Activity: "Tough Times"   **Page #:** 43   **Learning Type:** Collaborative
Description: Discuss the reactions that major and minor characters have to conflicts in the story. Decide what these reactions say about these characters.
Teacher Tip: Speaker 2's discussion question about a minor character may not apply if the story only really contains a main character. In this case, direct Speaker 2 to name a second conflict the main character faces and his/her reaction to it.

TEACHER INSTRUCTIONS (CONT.)

Activity: "The Structure of a Scene"   **Page #:** 44–45   **Learning Type:** Individual
Description: Learn about the classic plot structure and apply this concept to a scene from the novel. Then choose a scene that does not follow the classic plot structure and give textual reasons for why a nontraditional structure served the scene better.

Activity: "An Important Scene"   **Page #:** 46–47   **Learning Type:** Individual
Description: Highlight an important scene from the novel and examine the ingredients that were combined to create it. On the second page of this activity, consider an alternate ending for the scene and determine how this new ending would change the novel.

Activity: "Storyboard a Scene"   **Page #:** 48   **Learning Type:** Individual
Description: Use a storyboard to visually represent a scene from the novel. Explain why this particular scene lends itself well to being told visually.

Activity: "Timeline of Events"   **Page #:** 49   **Learning Type:** Individual
Description: Show the chronological sequence of events in the novel. Examine cause and effect by revealing how one event leads to another.

Activity: "Two Tales in One"   **Page #:** 50   **Learning Type:** Individual
Description: Track the individual events of two separate storylines. Use evidence from the text to show how the second storyline affects the main storyline.
Teacher Tip: Many novels feature two or more storylines that take place simultaneously and then meet up at a certain point. Use this activity for novels that fit this description — even if a second storyline is minor.

Activity: "All In Order"   **Page #:** 51   **Learning Type:** Individual
Description: Analyze the chronological order in which the novel is structured. Make and support a claim as to why the chosen time order best fits the story.

Activity: "I Predict" ↩   **Page #:** 52   **Learning Type:** Individual
Description: Make and defend two predictions about what will happen next in the novel.

Activity: "In the End"   **Page #:** 53   **Learning Type:** Individual
Description: Summarize and examine the closing scene(s) of the novel. Choose words to describe the ending, then support your choices with evidence from the text.

Activity: "Facts, Opinions, & Follow-Ups"   **Page #:** 54–56   **Learning Type:** Individual/Collaborative
Description: Report twice on an event that has taken place in the novel – when it first happens, and then after time has passed. Practice writing in two distinct formats: a newspaper article and a blog post. Discuss papers with partners.
Teacher Tip: This is a two-part activity. Students should complete the first writing after reading an early section of the novel. At that time, pair students and assign a different writing format to each partner. Later, have students revisit the event to show the latest effects of the event. Re-form the same student pairs for further discussion.

Activity: "Section Log-In"   **Page #:** 57   **Learning Type:** Individual
Description: Choose from several options to add to Interactive Novel Logs.

A Quick Guide to . . .

+ +

Plot → what happens in the story

Structure → the way that a story is ordered and organized

+ +

Elements in Action → from *Esperanza Rising* by Pam Muñoz Ryan

Plot	Structure
A girl grows up privileged and adored in Mexico. Tragedy soon strikes, and she and her mother are forced to flee to the United States. There, she is no longer treated like royalty, but instead she must adapt to hard labor and a life without the beautiful and comfortable things to which she has grown accustomed. She struggles to accept this new fate, but then her mother's illness forces her to grow up. After much struggle, she matures and becomes responsible. By the end of the novel, she is happy again. Her circumstances have changed, but she has learned to adapt to them.	The novel takes place over a year in the life of Esperanza and her family. It begins and ends on her birthday. It also begins and ends with the image of two people putting their heads to the ground to listen to the earth's heartbeat. Another structural element to this novel is the naming of the chapters. Each section is named after the crop being harvested at the time the chapter takes place. Once Esperanza becomes a laborer working in the fields, this structure strengthens the idea that her life and the lives of those around her are intertwined with the crops on which their survival depends.

Spotlight On → Conflict

Related Ideas: problem, complication, obstacle, struggle

One of the most important elements of any plot is **conflict**. Great novels contain at least one major conflict, although they may contain several. Conflict is what forces characters to change and grow as they struggle to overcome the obstacles they encounter.

There are several types of conflict. Here are four of the most common:

✦ **Person vs. Person** — A character struggles with another person or people in the story.

✦ **Person vs. Self** — A character struggles with his/her own emotions, thoughts, or feelings that create the problems in the story.

✦ **Person vs. Nature** — A character struggles with something in nature, such as the wilderness or a big storm.

✦ **Person vs. Society** — A character struggles against the beliefs, behaviors, and traditions of society.

NAME: _____

THE SUMMARIES OF ITS PARTS

As you finish reading each section of the novel, take a few minutes to summarize the events that took place in that section. Use the following tips to guide you:

✦ **Focus only on the most important events.** Do not include extra details or examples. A summary should be a quick retelling of only the major plot points.

✦ **Use your own words.** Do not quote words directly from the novel and do not rely on the novel's vocabulary.

✦ **Use transition words.** Words and phrases like *first*, *next*, *then*, *after that*, and *finally* quickly show the sequence in which events occur in the novel.

✦ + ✦ + ✦ + ✦ + ✦ + ✦ + ✦ + ✦ + ✦ + ✦ + ✦ + ✦ + ✦ + ✦ + ✦ + ✦ + ✦ + ✦ + ✦ +

Fit your section summary on the lines below.

Chapters in section: _____

Page numbers in section: *from page* _____ *to page* _____

_____

_____

_____

_____

_____

_____

_____

_____

_____

_____

_____

_____

In one or two complete sentences, name the single thing you found most interesting in this section. Your answer can be about something that happened in the plot, the way a character reacted to an event, or the way the author chose to write a particular line.

_____

_____

_____

MAJOR PLOT POINTS

Use the chart below to brainstorm a list of the most important events in each part of the novel.

✦ For each part, list three major events that happened in that part.

✦ For each event, explain why you consider it to be a major event in the novel. State how this event affects the rest of the novel.

Beginning	**Event #1:** Why it's important: **Event #2:** Why it's important: **Event #3:** Why it's important:
Middle	**Event #1:** Why it's important: **Event #2:** Why it's important: **Event #3:** Why it's important:
End	**Event #1:** Why it's important: **Event #2:** Why it's important: **Event #3:** Why it's important:

NAME: _____

IN THE BEGINNING

First impressions are very important. How to begin a novel is an important choice that an author must make. Answer the following questions about the beginning of this novel.

1. How does the novel begin? Describe the events of the first few pages.

_____

_____

_____

2. Describe the writing style of the first few pages. Is there a lot of description, dialogue, or action? Explain and give details.

_____

_____

_____

3. What mood or feeling is established in the first few pages?

_____

How does the author establish this mood? Give examples.

_____

_____

_____

4. Are there any signs or clues in these first few pages that tell you that the mood of the novel will change soon? If so, give examples. If not, do you think this mood will remain the same throughout most of the novel? Why?

_____

_____

_____

+ +

Considering Craft: Why do you think the author chose to start the book with this scene? What effect does it have on you as a reader? In what ways does this scene draw you into the book and make you want to read more?

_____

_____

_____

NAME(S): _____

GETTING TO KNOW A NOVEL

When you first begin a novel, you usually know nothing about it. The world of the novel is filled with people you have never met and places you have never been. An author must introduce you to that world and make you want to stay in it for a long time.

The first few pages of a novel often contain a lot of **exposition**. Exposition is information that helps you understand where you are in a story and who are the characters you are reading about. It is the background information you need to know in order to understand the characters, situations, and/or settings in the novel.

Work with a partner to answer these questions about the first few pages of the novel.

1. What exposition does the author give you about the characters you meet in those first pages?

   _____
   _____
   _____
   _____

   Is this information given mostly through description, dialogue, and/or actions?

   _____

2. What exposition does the author give you about the setting(s)?

   _____
   _____
   _____

   Is this information given mostly through description, dialogue, and/or actions?

   _____

3. What exposition does the author give you about the situation(s) the characters are in or the events that are happening?

   _____
   _____
   _____
   _____

   Is this information given mostly through description, dialogue, and/or actions?

   _____

NAME: _____

A QUARTET OF CONFLICTS

The **conflict** of the story is the problem the main character faces. Most stories have more than one conflict, but one is more important than the rest.

For this activity, think about four main types of conflict: **Person vs. Person**, **Person vs. Self**, **Person vs. Nature**, and **Person vs. Society**. Explain how each of these types of conflict occurs in the section of the novel you have just read. Also, find a quotation that shows evidence of each type of conflict. (Leave a box blank if you do not think that type of conflict is present in this section of the novel.)

+ +

Chapters or page numbers in section: _____

+ +

Person vs. Person Name the person or people who act(s) against the main character. Explain how this person or these people do this.	*Conflict(s):* *One quotation that shows this:* *Page number(s):*
Person vs. Self Name the thoughts, behaviors, or emotions the main character struggles to overcome.	*Conflict(s):* *One quotation that shows this:* *Page number(s):*
Person vs. Nature Name the forces of nature that act against the main character. Tell how this happens.	*Conflict(s):* *One quotation that shows this:* *Page number(s):*
Person vs. Society Explain how the attitudes and behaviors of the public cause conflict for the main character.	*Conflict(s):* *One quotation that shows this:* *Page number(s):*

TOUGH TIMES

It's hard to imagine a story that does not have **conflict**. The driving force behind most stories is the set of complications and struggles the characters encounter. Even comedies are built around conflict. They make us laugh because of the way the characters react to the problems they face.

For this activity, work with a partner. Begin by deciding who will speak first.

Speaker 1: _____
(name)

Speaker 2: _____
(name)

Answer this question aloud to your partner:

What is one major conflict the main character in the story faces? How does the main character react to this problem?

Listen to Speaker 1's answer. Discuss! Do you agree with, disagree with, or have anything to add to what was said?

then

Answer this question aloud to your partner:

What is one major conflict another (minor) character in the story faces? How does this character react to this problem?

Listen to Speaker 2's answer. Discuss! Do you agree with, disagree with, or have anything to add to what was said?

+ +

Time to Work Together

1. Think about the main character's reaction to the problem you two discussed. What does this reaction say about this main character? Explain.

_____

_____

_____

_____

_____

2. Think about the minor character's reaction to the problem you two discussed. What does this reaction say about this minor character? Explain.

_____

_____

_____

_____

NAME: _____

THE STRUCTURE OF A SCENE

Many novels — or scenes within them — follow a classic plot structure. This structure is made up of five basic parts, as the diagram below shows:

3. Climax
the moment of the most tension or excitement

2. Rising Action
the building of tension
or excitement

4. Falling Action
the decreasing of
tension or excitement

1. Exposition
the introduction of
information

5. Resolution
the ending or result
of the action

+ +

Think about the novel you are studying. Find a scene that you feel fits the classic plot structure, and use that scene to complete the chart below. In the **Climax** row, write the most exciting or tense moment of the scene. In the other rows, write two events that happen during those parts of the scene.

Quick description of scene: _____

_____ Page number(s): _____

Exposition how the basic situation is revealed		
Rising Action the events that set the scene in motion		
Climax the most exciting or tense moment		
Falling Action how the conflict begins to be resolved		
Resolution the end result of the action		

THE STRUCTURE OF A SCENE (CONT.)

Now choose another scene from the novel. Find one that you feel does not follow the classic plot structure. Examine this scene in detail.

Quick description of scene: _____

_____ Page number(s): _____

1. What, if any, exposition is included in this scene?

   _____

   _____

   _____

   _____

2. What was the scene's most exciting or tense moment?

   _____

   _____

   _____

3. What, if any, resolution was included in this scene?

   _____

   _____

4. Explain why you feel this scene did not follow the classic plot structure. Which parts of the classic plot structure were not included or were included in a different order?

   _____

   _____

   _____

   _____

5. Why do you think the author wrote this scene in this way? How was this scene better than it would have been if it had followed a more traditional structure?

   _____

   _____

   _____

   _____

   _____

NAME: _____

AN IMPORTANT SCENE

The plot is the series of events that make up the story. The author carefully creates events that show how the conflict or main problem of the story builds and resolves. Each point in the plot is important to the overall structure of the story.

Choose one important scene in the novel to analyze. Complete the form below.

Tell It Like It Is

What are the page numbers of this scene? _____

Which characters were involved? _____

Summarize what happens in this one scene.

_____

_____

_____

_____

_____

What caused the event in this scene? How did it happen?

_____

_____

_____

Find one quotation that is important to the scene.

_____

_____

_____ Page number(s): _____

Why is this an important scene? How does it fit within the whole story?

_____

_____

_____

_____

AN IMPORTANT SCENE (CONT.)

In the first part of this activity, you chose one event and explained why it is important to the overall story. Further explore this event and its impact on the overall novel.

Tell It Like It Could Have Been

How does that scene end? _____

_____

_____

Think of another way this scene could have ended. Describe the new ending here.

_____

_____

_____

_____

If the scene ended that way, how would the rest of the story change? Name three ways.

1. This new ending would have caused this to happen: _____

_____

Here's why: _____

2. This new ending would have caused this to happen: _____

_____

Here's why: _____

3. This new ending would have caused this to happen: _____

_____

Here's why: _____

Would this change make the story better or worse? Explain why. _____

_____

_____

_____

NAME: _____

STORYBOARD A SCENE

When movie directors think about how to film a scene, they often create a **storyboard**. They draw pictures of key moments in the scene to show how the action progresses within the scene.

Do this for an important scene from the novel. You may use a few words in or around each picture, but try to tell the story of the scene mostly through images.

1.	2.	3.
4.	5.	6.

Why did you choose this scene? What about the way this scene is written made you feel it was a good one to storyboard?

_____

_____

_____

NAME: _____

TIMELINE OF EVENTS

Use the chart below to show the sequence of events in the novel (or within a chapter, section, etc.). In the **When?** column, either write when the event happened (day, time, chapter) in the story or use transitional words (*first*, *next*, *then*, *after that*, *finally*) to show when the event happened in relation to the other events.

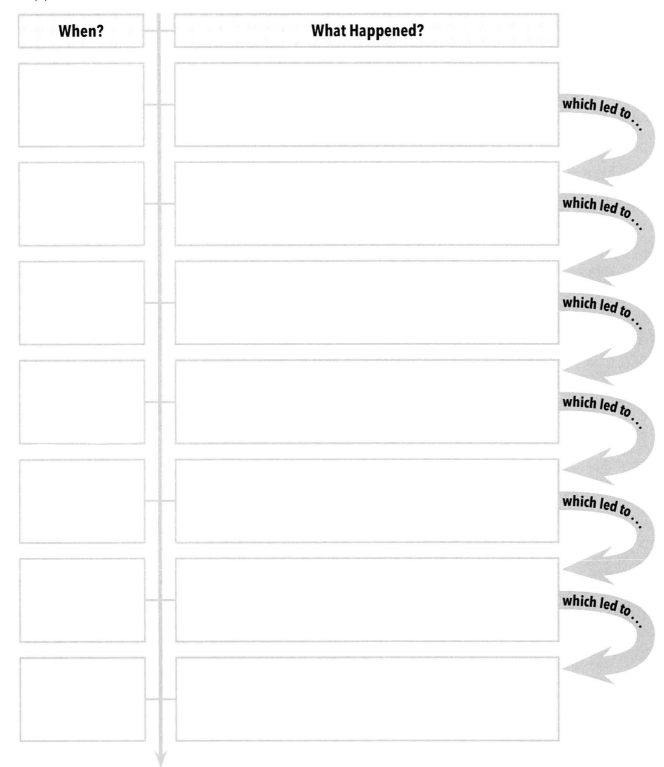

When?	What Happened?

which led to…

which led to…

which led to…

which led to…

which led to…

which led to…

NAME: _____

TWO TALES IN ONE

In the world of a novel — just like in our world — there is often more than one storyline to follow at a time. While a main character's storyline is featured, other characters have their own storylines and other events happen at the same time.

Use the diagram below to show how another of the novel's storylines is happening at the same time as the main one.

✦ Do the events of the other storyline affect the main storyline in any way? If so, jot some notes about how they do this.

✦ Do the storylines meet up at the end? If so, fill in the final box to show how the two storylines come together.

✦ ✦

Name of Novel: _____

Main Storyline	Other Storyline	Effect(s) on Main Storyline
		_____ _____ _____
		_____ _____ _____
		_____ _____ _____
		_____ _____ _____

50

NAME: _____

ALL IN ORDER

The events of most novels are written in **chronological** order. That means they are described in the same order as how they happened in the world of the novel. For this activity, think about the order of the events described in the novel.

1. How would you describe the events in this novel? (Check one box.)

   ☐ entirely in chronological order

   ☐ mostly in chronological order

   ☐ not in chronological order

2. Look at your answer to #1. Why do you think the author chose to order the events of the novel in this way? Why did this type of order make sense for the novel?

   _____

   _____

   _____

   _____

   _____

3. How would the novel have been changed if the author had put the events out of order chronologically? (Or if the events are already presented that way, how would the book have changed if the events had been given in chronological order?) Give two specific examples of how this would have changed the book.

   _____

   _____

   _____

   _____

   _____

   _____   **Remember!**

   _____   Include two
                                           examples from the
   _____   book to support
                                           your claim.

   _____

   _____

NAME: _____

I PREDICT

Now that you have read this section, where do you think the story will go next? Make two predictions based on what you have read so far. Your predictions can be about any aspects of plot (what will happen, why it will happen, to whom will it happen, etc.).

Cite details and evidence from previous sections to explain and defend each prediction.

+ +

Chapters or page numbers in section: _____

+ +

First Prediction

I predict this will happen: _____

_____

_____

_____

_____

Here is why I predict this: _____

_____

_____

_____

_____

Second Prediction

I predict this will happen: _____

_____

_____

_____

_____

Here is why I predict this: _____

_____

_____

_____

_____

NAME: _____

IN THE END

The ending of a book should follow logically from the sequence of events in the story. On this page, examine the ending of the novel.

1. How does the novel end? Write a brief summary.

_____

_____

_____

_____

_____

2. Do the events at the end of the novel fit with what happened in the story? Explain.

_____

_____

_____

3. Choose three words to describe the ending of the novel. For each, give examples from the book that show why you chose that word.

Word #1: _____ Evidence: _____

_____

_____

Word #2: _____ Evidence: _____

_____

_____

Word #3: _____ Evidence: _____

_____

_____

4. Choose one minor character that you would want to know more about. What do you think might happen to this minor character in the future? Give reasons from the book for why you feel this way.

_____

_____

_____

NAME(S): _____

FACTS, OPINIONS, & FOLLOW-UPS

News travels fast these days. News reporters are expected to have the facts about an event within minutes of it happening. At the same time, bloggers post their thoughts and opinions on the Internet when just about any sort of event happens.

Newspaper articles and blog posts both deal with the reporting of information, but they go about it in different ways.

Newspaper Articles   **Both**   **Blog Posts**

+ only facts
+ answer the 5Ws and 1H
+ professional writing tone
+ printed on paper (daily, weekly, etc.)

+ include a catchy headline
+ can include picture(s)
+ can be posted online

+ personal thoughts and opinions
+ written with personality
+ posted as often as needed

+ +

Think about an important event from the novel. Imagine you are a reporter who lives in the world of the novel. How would you describe the event?

First Write either a newspaper article or a blog post about the event. Your teacher will assign you one or the other.

Next Exchange your article/post with a partner.

Then Read your partner's writing. Then meet with him or her to discuss each other's work aloud. Complete these sentence starters:

One thing my partner's article did well was _____.

Here is why: _____.

One thing I feel my partner could have included or done differently was _____ _____. *Here is why:* _____.

Later After you have read more sections of the novel, use the new information that you now have to write a follow-up article about the same event. This time, use the format — newspaper article or blog post — that you *did not* use the first time.

Finally Exchange papers with a partner once more and discuss the new articles.

This time, one thing my partner's article did well was _____.

Here is why: _____.

This time, one thing I feel my partner could have included or done differently was _____. *Here is why:* _____.

FACTS, OPINIONS, & FOLLOW-UPS (CONT.)

NEWSPAPER ARTICLE

Use the template below to write a newspaper article about an event from the novel.

✦ Include the name of the newspaper at the very top of the page and a headline for the story at the top of the article.

✦ If possible, answer the **5Ws** and **1H** (Who, What, When, Where, Why, and How) about the event you are describing.

✦ Decide what kind of picture might be included in an article like this and draw/paste one in the space provided.

NAME: _____

FACTS, OPINIONS, & FOLLOW-UPS (CONT.)

ONLINE BLOG

Use the template below to write a blog post about an event from the novel.

✦ Include the name of your blog at the very top of the page. Above your post, add a headline.

✦ Create a design for the border of your page. You can add a picture at the top, bottom, and/or around the edges. You can add links, tabs, or any other design feature you might normally see on web pages.

✦ Decide what kind of picture might be included with an entry like this and draw/paste one in the space provided.

SECTION LOG-IN

Use the prompts below to make a more personal connection to what you have read. Choose one of the following suggestions and use it to fill a page in your Interactive Novel Log. Take this opportunity to connect to the novel in a way that interests you.

Begin by reading each idea. Put a checkmark beside the ones that most appeal to you.

+ +

Ideas for Your Interactive Novel Log

☐ **Tweet It!** — Write a series of four tweets. In the first three, offer a quick insight into what happens in the beginning, the middle, and then the end of the novel. In the last tweet, give your overall impression of the whole novel. Each tweet can be no more than 140 characters in length.

☐ **If It Were Me** — Imagine you are stuck in the world of the novel. Which event from the novel would be the most challenging (or enjoyable, frustrating, etc.) for you to deal with? Why?

☐ **Plot the Plot** — Create a line graph showing what you feel were the most exciting and least exciting points in the novels. Show two of each, and explain why you felt this way as you were reading.

☐ **The Turning Point** — Novels often have a turning point, a moment when something happens that changes everything for the main character. What was your turning point as you read this novel? What one moment made you suddenly realize that you were going to really like (or really not like) this novel? Name the moment and explain why it had such an effect on you.

☐ **Years From Now** — Based on the events of the story, what do you think will happen to the characters in the future? Create a chart in which you imagine the lives of each character at various points (5 years, 10 years, etc.) in the future.

☐ **Déjà Vu** — Did any of the events from this novel remind you of the events from a different novel or film? Write a paragraph or create a chart comparing the two pieces of art. Which one was better, in your opinion? Why?

☐ **It's New to Me** — What one event from the novel's plot is something you have never read about in any book before or seen in any film? Write about that part of the plot and explain your thoughts about it.

☐ **Other** — Come up with an idea of your own! Your idea should be related to the concept of plot or to the specific plot of the novel you are reading.

_____

_____

TEACHER INSTRUCTIONS

The term **setting** refers not only to *where* a story takes place but also *when*. **Genre** refers to the literary category (e.g., Western, fantasy, sci-fi) in which a novel fits based on the elements contained within it.

Distribute "A Quick Guide to . . ." (page 59), which gives an overview and examples of setting and genre, along with an in-depth look at a key term. You may also have students consult the "Glossary of Literary Terms" resource (page 140) to reference related literary terms.

+ +

As your students read the novel, use the following worksheets to help them analyze and examine aspects related to setting and genre.

⟲ *Activities marked with this icon are meant to be used after the reading of each section of the novel. At that time, distribute fresh copies of these pages. Completed copies should be included in each student's Interactive Novel Log.*

Activity: "Location, Location" ⟲   **Page #:** 60   **Learning Type:** Collaborative
Description: List all of the settings in the novel and sort them into categories. Practice speaking and listening by choosing the most important locations and defending choices.

Activity: "A Place of Meaning"   **Page #:** 61   **Learning Type:** Individual
Description: Explore the deeper connections characters have with settings in the novel.

Activity: "A Sense of Place"   **Page #:** 62-63   **Learning Type:** Individual/Collaborative
Description: Examine how the author uses sensory words to give readers an understanding of setting.
Teacher Tip: The second page of this activity will work best for groups of three or four.

Activity: "Where It Begins and Ends"   **Page #:** 64   **Learning Type:** Individual
Description: Analyze the importance of the settings in the beginning and ending of the novel. Show how these two settings bookend the novel and give clues to its overall arc.

Activity: "Seasons and Weather"   **Page #:** 65   **Learning Type:** Individual
Description: Consider the role of seasons and weather in the novel and how these elements affect characters and/or plot.

Activity: "Time Period"   **Page #:** 66   **Learning Type:** Collaborative
Description: Locate clues that show the time period of the novel. Theorize how an alternate time period would affect the characters and plot of the novel.

Activity: "The Passage of Time"   **Page #:** 67   **Learning Type:** Individual
Description: Think about how time passes during the novel and the effects this has on the plot, characters, etc.

Activity: "Name the Genre"   **Page #:** 68   **Learning Type:** Individual
Description: Determine the primary genre of the novel, along with any subgenres.
Teacher Tip: For this activity, each student will need a dark marker, a highlighter, and a copy of "List of Fiction Genres" (page 141).

Activity: "A Different Genre"   **Page #:** 69   **Learning Type:** Individual
Description: Reimagine the novel in a different genre, and then rewrite a scene or provide a summary.

Activity: "Section Log-In"   **Page #:** 70   **Learning Type:** Individual
Description: Choose from several options to add to Interactive Novel Logs.

A QUICK GUIDE TO . . .

+ +

Setting → where and when a story takes place

Genre → the category into which a novel fits based on its characters, settings, and conflicts

+ +

Elements in Action → from *Holes* by Louis Sachar

Setting	Genre
The main setting of the novel *Holes* is Camp Green Lake, a dry, dusty desert with no lake and nothing green. The hot weather and isolated location play an important role in the plot. Much of the story takes place in the present time, but there are several scenes that take place at various times in the past, as well.	This story fits into a few categories, or genres. It has many elements common to the genre of children's literature (such as buried treasure, difficult journeys, unpleasant adult characters). It also is an example of the genre of magical realism. Most of the elements in the world of *Holes* are realistic, but the author sprinkles in a few things that are a bit too incredible for the real world (for example, yellow-spotted lizards, family curses, and the magic power of onions).

Spotlight On → **Nonfiction vs. Historical Fiction**

Related Ideas: genre, point of view, historical figures, events from history

A piece of writing is nonfiction if it only contains facts and describes real events. Examples of the books that fit into the nonfiction genre are biographies and autobiographies. These books attempt to tell true stories about real people who live or have lived in our real world.

Novels are works of fiction. At least some parts of novels have been made up by the author. However, novels can include real people or describe real events. The best example of this is **historical fiction**. A novel that fits into the genre of historical fiction does the following things:

✓ It is set in the past.

✓ The setting should look like it did at that point in history.

✓ The people should dress, act, and speak like people did in that place at that time in history.

✓ It often includes real historical figures — people we know lived back then and did certain things.

✓ It also includes characters who were created by the author. These characters interact with or observe the historical figures. The story is often told from the point of view of one of these fictitious (made up) characters.

NAME(S): _____

LOCATION, LOCATION

With a partner, list the different places that are described in this section of the novel. Where does the action take place? Think about big settings (such as cities) and small settings (such as someone's room). Think about indoor settings and outdoor ones, too. See how many you can name.

+ +

Chapters or page numbers in section: _____

+ +

Settings from _____ ← *(name of novel)*

Big	Small	Indoor	Outdoor

Each partner should choose a different setting that is very important to this section of the novel. Discuss.

Partner 1: _____
(name)

Partner 2: _____
(name)

Answer this question aloud and support your opinion with reasons:

*I think **[name of big or small setting]** is one of the most important settings because **[reasons from novel]**.*

Listen to Partner 1's answer. On the back of this paper, write a summary of your partner's answer.

then

Answer this question aloud and support your opinion with reasons:

*I think **[name of an indoor or outdoor setting]** is another of the most important settings because **[reasons from novel]**.*

Listen to Partner 2's answer. On the back of this paper, write a summary of your partner's answer.

+ +

Discuss with your partner: Are these two settings more similar or different in how they're important to the novel? On the back of this paper, write a brief summary of your discussion.

A PLACE OF MEANING

For this activity, think about setting as it relates to characters in this novel. Choose two characters, and then match each character to a setting that has special significance for that character. Try to go beyond simple connections; instead, try to find deep connections that you can support with evidence from the novel.

Examples:

Simple	Deeper
Character A is connected to Setting A because it was once her home.	Character A is connected to Setting A because that is the last place where she saw her father, and this setting represents the childhood that she feels she has lost forever.

+ +

Connection #1   Name of Character: _____

Name of Setting: _____

Why does this setting have special meaning for this character?

_____

_____

_____

_____

Quotation or example from novel: _____

_____

_____ Page number(s): _____

Connection #2   Name of Character: _____

Name of Setting: _____

Why does this setting have special meaning for this character?

_____

_____

_____

_____

Quotation or example from novel: _____

_____

_____ Page number(s): _____

NAME: _____

A SENSE OF PLACE

Authors use descriptive language to make settings come to life. For this activity, examine an interesting passage from the novel. This passage should contain a lot of detailed, descriptive language that appeals to the senses. Complete the following chart.

Name of Novel	
Page Numbers of Passage	
Where does this passage take place?	
What is happening in this passage? Write a summary.	
Find words and phrases that describe images that appeal to the senses.	See: Hear: Touch: Taste: Smell:

62

A SENSE OF PLACE (CONT.)

For this activity, use the chart you completed on the previous page. Work in groups of three or four. Discuss the following questions as a group. For each question, give a brief recap of your group's answer. Then give any additional thoughts that you have about the question. For example, do you agree or disagree with your group's response, and why?

To begin, each group member should identify the passage he or she examined and should list some of the sensory words the author used in that passage.

Member's Name	Passage Examined	Sensory Words

1. Think about how the sensory words and phrases help the reader understand the setting of the passage. In this way, what are some things that these passages have in common? How are they different in their use of sensory words?

   Group's Answer: _____

   _____

   More Thoughts: _____

   _____

2. Now think about the mood or feeling that these sensory words give to each passage. What feeling does the descriptive language add to each passage?

   Group's Answer: _____

   _____

   More Thoughts: _____

   _____

3. In the opinion of your group, which passage best uses sensory images to make the reader feel the action and/or setting of the scene? Why?

   Group's Answer: _____

   _____

   More Thoughts: _____

   _____

NAME: _____

WHERE IT BEGINS AND ENDS

The setting in which an author chooses to begin a novel can have significance. It can give us clues to the events and lives of the characters before the novel begins. Take a closer look at where the novel begins, where it ends, and the significance of these two locations. (**Note:** If the beginning and ending settings are the same, this can also be significant.)

1. Describe the setting in which the novel begins.

_____

_____

_____

2. What does this setting tell us about the main character's life before the novel begins?

_____

_____

3. What significance does this opening setting have to the rest of the novel? Explain.

_____

_____

4. Describe the setting in which the novel ends.

_____

_____

_____

5. How do the events in the novel get the main character from the opening setting to the ending setting?

_____

_____

_____

6. How does the ending setting show a change (or lack of change) in the life of the main character?

_____

_____

7. What do you think the ending setting tells us about the near future for the main character?

_____

_____

SEASONS AND WEATHER

In many novels, nature plays an important role. The season(s) and weather can affect the actions and emotions of characters. These elements can cause both major and minor events that impact the novel in important ways.

1. Describe the season(s) in which the novel takes place. _____

_____

2. Describe any weather that impacts or affects the characters or events in the novel.

Type of Weather	Effect on Character/Events

3. Why do you think the author chose to set the novel during this particular season or include these types of weather? What do these choices add to the mood of the novel?

_____

_____

_____

4. How would the novel have been different if it had taken place in the opposite season or included other types of weather?

_____

_____

_____

In your opinion, would this change have been for the better or worse? Why?

_____

_____

_____

NAME(S): _____

TIME PERIOD

The term **setting** describes not only *where* a piece of writing takes place but also *when*. The time period in which a novel is set can be a very important element that helps you understand its characters and events. Work with a partner to consider the idea of *when* this novel takes place.

1. What is the time period of this novel? Circle one.

in the past   **in the future**   **in our current time**

2. What clues help you determine the time period of this novel? Complete the chart.

Clues	Examples
Objects (technology, etc.)	
Culture (art, speech, etc.)	
Style (clothes, etc.)	

3. Think about how the novel would be different if it were set in a different time.

✦ **If the novel is set in the future or the current time:** How would the novel need to change if it were set 100 years ago? Give three specific examples.

✦ **If the novel is set in the past:** How would the novel need to change if it were set in today's world? Give three specific examples.

_____

_____

_____

_____

_____

4. Think about your answer to question #3. Could the novel work in this new time period? Or would it have to be too different? Explain.

_____

_____

_____

THE PASSAGE OF TIME

Some novels take place within a very short period of time, while others span longer periods. Think about how much time passes in the world of the novel you are reading.

1. Describe the time (day, month, year, season, etc.) at the beginning of the novel.

   _____

2. Describe the time (day, month, year, season, etc.) at the end of the novel.

   _____

3. How much time passes from the beginning of the novel until the end?

   _____

   What important events (holidays, school events, etc.) show the passage of time within the novel?

   _____

4. Find two passages/scenes that are separated by a short period of time.

   Describe each: _____

   _____

   _____

   _____

   Why is it important that only a short time passes between the two? _____

   _____

5. Find two passages/scenes that are separated by a much longer period of time.

   Describe each: _____

   _____

   _____

   _____

   Why is it important that a longer time passes between these two? _____

   _____

6. Give some thoughts about why the author chose this time frame for the novel. How does it add to the mood, themes, or conflicts?

   _____

   _____

   _____

NAME: _____

NAME THE GENRE

In literature, the word *genre* refers to the category a novel fits into. Books that fit into a certain genre usually share similar forms, style, settings, or subject matter. Here is a list of genres:

adventure	**fairy tale**	**realistic**
contemporary	**historical**	**science fiction**
fantasy	**magical realism**	**suspense**

For this activity, you will need a dark marker and a yellow highlighter. Read the chart below. Black out or highlight the above genre boxes according to the directions given in the chart.

Question	*If answer to question is "Yes," do this →*	**Black Out**	**Highlight**
Do most of the events in the novel take place in the present time?		*historical, science fiction*	*contemporary, realistic*
Do most of the events in the novel take place in the past?		*contemporary, science fiction*	*historical*
Do most of the events in the novel take place in the future?		*historical, contemporary*	*science fiction*
Does all of the technology in the story exist right now, and is it regularly used in today's world?		*historical, science fiction, fantasy*	*contemporary, realistic*
Can everything that happens in the story be explained by the rules of the world in which we live in?		*science fiction, fantasy, magical realism*	*realistic*
Is the story set in a completely different world, filled mostly with different beings, etc.?		*realism, contemporary, historical*	*fantasy*

Using your answers from the chart and also what you know about the genres, which would you say is the primary genre of this novel?

Explain. _____

_____

_____

Are there any other genres into which this novel also fits? Explain. _____

_____

_____

NAME: _____

A DIFFERENT GENRE

Imagine this novel had been written in a completely different genre. The new version of the novel would have many of the same characters, settings, themes, etc., but it would incorporate elements of the new genre.

First Choose and check one of the following genres. Be sure to choose one that is *not* the genre of the actual novel.

☐ adventure ☐ fantasy ☐ historical

☐ magical realism ☐ science fiction ☐ Western

Next Choose and check one of the following tasks.

☐ **Rewrite a short scene from the new novel.**

☐ **Write a summary of the new novel.**

+ +

_____

_____

_____

_____

_____

_____

_____

_____

_____

_____

_____

_____

_____

_____

_____

_____

_____

NAME: _____

SECTION LOG-IN

Use the prompts below to make a more personal connection to what you have read. Choose one of the following suggestions and use it to fill a page in your Interactive Novel Log. Take this opportunity to connect to the novel in a way that interests you.

Begin by reading each idea. Put a checkmark beside the ones that most appeal to you.

+ +

Ideas for Your Interactive Novel Log

☐ **First Day** — Imagine that you have just moved to the place (and/or time period) where the novel is set. How will you adjust to this new setting? Describe your first day.

☐ **Welcome Mat** — Imagine that the main character from the novel will be moving to your town or city. Write a short statement welcoming this person to your area. Also create two lists: one that tells the characters the things about your city that will make him or her feel right at home, and then another that names the things he or she will have to get used to. Base these lists on what you know about the character and also about your area.

☐ **Fit In, Stand Out** — Think about the world of the novel. Which objects, characters, or ideas from that world would fit right into the world you live in? Which would stand out as being completely different from anything in your world?

☐ **The Feel of a Place** — Think of a place in the novel where a character had a specific feeling (such as comfort, sadness, or excitement). Write about a place that gives you a similar feeling. Compare your experiences in your place with those of the character in his or hers.

☐ **Weather Watch** — Does weather play an important role in the novel? Create a 5-day weather forecast for the area featured in the novel. Pretend you are a meteorologist. Explain how the weather will affect the people and places in the novel.

☐ **Cloud Clusters** — Create two word clouds for the novel: one for *where* it is set, and one for *when* it is set. Think of words related to these two ideas. Arrange these words to make cloud-like shapes. Make the words naming the main places and times the largest. See the example to the right.

☐ **Genre Mash-Up** — If you could insert one element from a different genre into this story, which would you choose? Would you give someone a time machine? Would a historical figure move in next door to the main character? Would a crime be committed that must be solved? Describe the element. Explain how it would alter the novel.

☐ **Other** — Come up with an idea of your own! Your idea should be related to the concepts of setting or genre or to the specific places in the novel you are reading.

_____

_____

TEACHER INSTRUCTIONS

The terms **main idea** and **theme** are very similar and often cause confusion for students. It is important to distinguish these terms and give students practice in locating each within texts.

✦ **Main idea** refers to what happens in the story. It is a statement that sums up the big idea of the novel (or any part within it). <u>The main idea is usually given in one sentence.</u>

✦ **Theme** describes the underlying message(s) or lesson(s) that the author wants the reader to take from the story. <u>The theme is usually named with one word or a short phrase.</u>

Distribute "A Quick Guide to . . ." (page 72), which gives an overview and examples of main idea and theme, along with an in-depth look at a key term. You may also have students consult the "Glossary of Literary Terms" resource (page 140) to reference related literary terms.

✦ ✦

As your students read the novel, use the following worksheets to help them analyze and examine aspects related to main idea and theme.

↺ *Activities marked with this icon are meant to be used after the reading of each section of the novel. At that time, distribute fresh copies of these pages. Completed copies should be included in each student's Interactive Novel Log.*

Activity: "What's the Big Idea?" ↺   **Page #:** 73   **Learning Type:** Individual
Description: Name the major events in one section of the novel and consider how those events are connected. Determine the main idea.

Activity: "List of Common Themes"   **Page #:** 74   **Learning Type:** Individual
Description: Look at a list of common themes. Annotate the list to clear up difficult terms or to point out themes that are present in the novel being studied.

Activity: "Checking In on Theme" ↺   **Page #:** 75   **Learning Type:** Individual
Description: Choose two themes that are present in the section of the novel you have just read. Decide why this theme is important, and give evidence to show how the author included it.
Teacher Tip: Distribute copies of "List of Common Themes" (page 74) before beginning this activity.

Activity: "Theme vs. Main Idea"   **Page #:** 76   **Learning Type:** Individual
Description: Think about the themes and main ideas of the entire novel. Name three themes and the main ideas that correspond to them. Cite evidence.

Activity: "A Tale of Two Chapters"   **Page #:** 77   **Learning Type:** Collaborative
Description: Practice speaking and listening skills. Compare and contrast the author's use of theme in two chapters or scenes.
Teacher Tip: If possible, find several pairs of chapters/scenes that work well for this activity and assign each member of each group a different chapter or scene.

Activity: "This About Covers It"   **Page #:** 78   **Learning Type:** Individual
Description: Look closely at the cover art and title to determine the clues they give to the themes presented in the novel.

Activity: "Section Log-In"   **Page #:** 79   **Learning Type:** Individual
Description: Choose from several options to add to Interactive Novel Logs.

A QUICK GUIDE TO . . .

✦ ✦

Main Idea → what the story is mostly about
(written in one sentence)

Theme → the story's message or lesson
(written in one word or a very short phrase)

✦ ✦

Elements in Action → from *Hatchet* by Gary Paulsen

Main Idea	Theme
The main idea of the novel *Hatchet* can be summed up as follows:	Over the course of this novel, the author explores many themes, including the following:

Main Idea

The main idea of the novel *Hatchet* can be summed up as follows:

> After being the sole survivor of a plane crash, a young boy is forced to survive in the Canadian wilderness for 54 days. During this time, he learns to respect this new environment and to adapt to its way of life.

Theme

Over the course of this novel, the author explores many themes, including the following:

▲ the natural world
▲ survival
▲ adaptation
▲ coexistence
▲ patience
▲ perseverance
▲ isolation
▲ transformation
▲ family
▲ memory
▲ wisdom and knowledge

Spotlight On → Theme

Related Ideas: big idea, lesson, message

A theme is a message behind what happens in the story. It can usually be described in one word or with a very short phrase.

Many stories have one major theme and several minor themes. A major theme is a big idea that is present throughout the entire novel. The plot and the characters of the novel in some way shed light on the major theme the author is trying to show his or her readers.

When trying to determine a theme of a novel, think about these questions:

✓ Why is the story important?

✓ What does it teach us or show us about life?

✓ What are the big ideas that hold the story together?

WHAT'S THE BIG IDEA?

Think about the main idea(s) of the section you have just read.

+ +

Chapters or page numbers in section: _____

+ +

What happens?

Name the three most major events that occur in this part of the novel.

1. _____

2. _____

3. _____

How are these events related?

Think about how these three events are related. Can you find connections between all three (or at least two of the three)? List those connections here.

_____

_____

_____

_____

So what's the big idea?

Add up what you've learned about this section to determine the main idea of this part of the novel. The main idea is a brief description (usually one sentence) that tells you what the author most wants you think about or take from this part of the novel.

Main Idea: _____

_____

What evidence (examples, quotations) from the novel can you give to support your answer?

_____

_____

_____

If you believe there is another main idea also included in this section, list it here and explain.

_____

_____

_____

NAME: _____

LIST OF COMMON THEMES

There are many themes that are common to children's and young-adult literature. The list below provides several.

If you think of more, add them to the list. If there are any terms you don't understand, consult a teacher, classmate, or dictionary. In the area beside each difficult term, you may write a note to remind you of its meaning.

	NOTES		NOTES
☐ Abandonment		☐ Illness	
☐ Acceptance		☐ Innocence	
☐ Bullying		☐ Justice/Judgment	
☐ Coming of Age		☐ Loneliness	
☐ Communication		☐ Memory/the Past	
☐ Compassion/Forgiveness		☐ Mortality	
☐ Courage		☐ Nature	
☐ Creativity		☐ Perseverance	
☐ Death and Loss		☐ Poverty/Wealth	
☐ Family		☐ Prejudice/Racism	
☐ Fate		☐ Rebellion	
☐ Fear		☐ Rules and Order	
☐ Fitting In		☐ Society and Class	
☐ Free Will		☐ Survival	
☐ Friendship		☐ Teamwork	
☐ Gender Issues		☐ Tradition/Customs	
☐ Hopes and Dreams		☐ Transformation	
☐ Identity		☐ Wisdom/Knowledge	

NAME: _____

CHECKING IN ON THEME

Most novels contain several themes that appear and reappear throughout. Look at your "List of Common Themes" handout. Choose two themes that you think are very important to this section of the novel.

+ +

Chapters or page numbers in section: _____

+ +

Theme #1: _____

Why do you think this theme is important in this section?

_____

_____

Give at least one example from the novel that shows this theme.

_____

_____

_____

Theme #2: _____

Why do you think this theme is important in this section?

_____

_____

Give at least one example from the novel that shows this theme.

_____

_____

_____

Of the two themes listed above, would you say that one of those is the major theme of the section? Why do you consider this theme to be more important to this part of the novel than the other one?

_____

_____

_____

_____

NAME: _____

THEME VS. MAIN IDEA

Use this worksheet to think about the main ideas and themes of the entire novel. Think of three themes that are important to this novel. For each one, state the main idea that is being conveyed by this theme and explain how the story shows this theme.

	Theme vs.	Main Idea	
What It Means	The **THEME** is the underlying **message** or **lesson** that the author wants the reader to take from the story.	The **MAIN IDEA** is mostly **what the story is about**.	
Clue	A theme can usually be given in one word (such as "Survival") or in a very short sentence (such as "It's okay to be different").	The main idea should be given in one sentence.	**How the Story Shows this Theme**
Theme #1			
Theme #2			
Theme #3			

A TALE OF TWO CHAPTERS

Work with a partner on this activity. You and your partner should each reread a different chapter or important scene from the novel. Then discuss each part. Listen to your partner and use his or her words to complete the questions below. Remember . . .

✦ **To name the <u>main idea</u> of a chapter or scene**, write one sentence that sums up the entire chapter or scene.

✦ **To name the <u>theme</u> of a chapter or scene**, write one word (or a short phrase) that names the lesson or message of the chapter or scene.

✦ ✦

Listen and Record

Which chapter or scene did your partner talk about? _____

What are three events that happen in this chapter or scene?

1. _____

2. _____

3. _____

What did your partner say is the main idea of this chapter or scene? _____

_____

What did your partner say is the theme of this chapter or scene? _____

Give Your Opinion

Do you agree with your partner about the main idea of the chapter or scene? Explain.

_____

Do you agree with your partner about the theme of the chapter or scene? Explain.

_____

Work Together

What is one way your chosen scene and your partner's scene are similar in their themes?

_____

_____

What is one way your chosen scene and your partner's scene are different in their themes?

_____

_____

NAME: _____

THIS ABOUT COVERS IT

Novels give you information before you even open them. For this activity, take a look at the cover and title of the book. These are the first things you see and read when you pick up a book, and they are often the first clue to the themes inside.

1. What is the title written on the front of the novel?

   _____

2. How does this title relate to what happens on the pages of the novel?

   _____

   _____

   _____

3. Think about the title and how it relates to theme. What themes are suggested by this title? What messages or big ideas does this title make you think of?

   _____

   _____

   _____

   Why does this title make you think of these things?

   _____

   _____

4. What are the colors, images, and letter styles used on the cover of the book?

   _____

   _____

5. How do these colors, images, or styles relate to what happens on the pages of the novel?

   _____

   _____

6. Are there any themes or big ideas that are suggested by the colors or pictures on the cover of this novel? Explain your answer.

   _____

   _____

   _____

   _____

78

NAME: _____

SECTION LOG-IN

Use the prompts below to make a more personal connection to what you have read. Choose one of the following suggestions and use it to fill a page in your Interactive Novel Log. Take this opportunity to connect to the novel in a way that interests you.

Begin by reading each idea. Put a checkmark beside the ones that most appeal to you.

+ +

Ideas for Your Interactive Novel Log

☐ **Inside Outside** — Many children's or young-adult novels include the theme of fitting in. An important character is often someone who is an outsider and must find a way to be accepted by a new group. Compare and contrast a character's experience with one of your own. Maybe there was a time when you were on the outside trying to fit in. Or maybe there was a time when you were on the inside observing another person trying to fit in.

☐ **Part of a Team** — Many children's or young-adult novels include the theme of teamwork or being a part of a group. What are your experiences with being on a team? How do those experiences relate to the experiences of the characters in the novel? Compare and contrast these two sets of experiences.

☐ **Overcoming Obstacles** — Many children's or young-adult novels include the theme of overcoming obstacles or perseverance (working hard to achieve something even though you don't have immediate success). How does this theme relate to your experiences? Compare and contrast your experiences of overcoming obstacles with those of a character in the novel.

☐ **Top 2** — Look back at the "List of Common Themes" handout. Think about the books and movies that you like the most. Do you notice any themes that seem to show up often in your favorite books, movies, or songs? Choose two themes from the list that are common to your favorite books, films, music, etc. Are these two themes similar to each other or different? Give reasons why these themes might have extra appeal for you. If you want, give examples of the books, movies, or songs that feature these themes.

☐ **Bottom 2** — Look back at the "List of Common Themes" handout. Do you notice any themes that don't usually appeal to you in books, movies, or songs? Choose two such themes. Are they very similar to each other or different? Give reasons why you think you do not tend to like books, movies, or songs that are based on these themes. If you want, give examples of books, movies, or songs that feature these themes.

☐ **Other** — Come up with an idea of your own! Your idea should be related to the concepts of main idea or theme or to the specific themes in the novel you are reading.

_____

_____

Author's Craft

TEACHER INSTRUCTIONS

The term **author's craft** refers to the tools an author uses to form a piece of literature.

Distribute "A Quick Guide to . . ." (page 82), which gives an overview and examples of author's craft, along with an in-depth look at a key term. You may also have students consult the "Glossary of Literary Terms" resource (page 140) to reference related literary terms.

+ +

As your students read the novel, use the following worksheets to help them analyze and examine aspects related to author's craft.

🔄 *Activities marked with this icon are meant to be used after the reading of each section of the novel. At that time, distribute fresh copies of these pages. Completed copies should be included in each student's Interactive Novel Log.*

Activity: "The Long and Short of It" 🔄 **Page #:** 83 **Learning Type:** Individual
Description: Examine how the author varies sentence, paragraph, and chapter length. Determine the effects of these choices on the story and the reader's experience.

Activity: "Form Flip" **Page #:** 84 **Learning Type:** Individual
Description: Learn about writing forms and determine the form in which the novel is written. Imagine a scene or passage in an alternate form and decide how a change in form would have affected the novel as a whole.

Activity: "Beginnings and Endings" 🔄 **Page #:** 85 **Learning Type:** Individual
Description: Look closely at how chapters begin and end. Choose one beginning and one ending to analyze. Make a claim as to why these authorial choices were effective.

Activity: "Explicit vs. Implicit" **Page #:** 86 **Learning Type:** Individual
Description: Analyze specific quotations and determine the literal information they give, as well as the information that can be inferred from them.
Teacher Tip: Before beginning, locate quotations that work well for this activity. Model one quotation, showing students how it works both explicitly and implicitly.

Activity: "Meanings to the Ends" **Page #:** 87 **Learning Type:** Individual
Description: Consider the questions implied by the endings of chapters. Study how authors use implication to create questions and thoughts in readers' minds. Locate an ending that provides literal information, as well.

Activity: "Painting a Picture" **Page #:** 88 **Learning Type:** Individual
Description: Show how an author uses descriptive language to form a picture of the settings as well as the characters in a scene.

Activity: "Descriptive Discussion" **Page #:** 89 **Learning Type:** Collaborative
Description: Discuss the author's use of imagery. Practice listening to partners and paraphrasing spoken information.
Teacher Tip: This collaborative activity builds off the previous individual activity ("Painting a Picture") and should be used in conjunction with it.

TEACHER INSTRUCTIONS (CONT.)

Activity: "Tone vs. Mood"   **Page #:** 90   **Learning Type:** Collaborative
Description: Compare and contrast the tone and mood of the novel. Work with a partner to defend and discuss claims.

Activity: "Making the Mood" ↩   **Page #:** 91   **Learning Type:** Individual
Description: Determine how an author combines such elements as plot, setting, characterization, voice, and dialogue to create the mood of a scene.

Activity: "So to Speak"   **Page #:** 92   **Learning Type:** Individual
Description: Compare and contrast two exchanges of dialogue involving the main character. Decide how these exchanges reveal the main character's personality, as well as how he/she interacts with other characters.

Activity: "Speaking of Dialogue"   **Page #:** 93   **Learning Type:** Collaborative
Description: Practice speaking and listening skills while making, supporting, and defending claims about how dialogue reveals character in the novel.
Teacher Tip: This collaborative activity builds off the previous individual activity ("So to Speak") and should be used in conjunction with it.

Activity: "Oh, the Irony"   **Page #:** 94   **Learning Type:** Individual
Description: Learn about three types of irony and find examples of each in the novel.

Activity: "More Than Meets the Eye"   **Page #:** 95   **Learning Type:** Collaborative
Description: Work with a partner to locate examples of symbolism. Discuss and defend choices to show how one person, one place, and one object function as symbols in the novel.

Activity: "Left in Suspense" ↩   **Page #:** 96   **Learning Type:** Individual
Description: Examine cliffhangers — how they are created, what purpose they serve, and what effect they have on the reader.

Activity: "In the Past, In the Future"   **Page #:** 97   **Learning Type:** Individual
Description: Find an example of either flashback or foreshadowing. Describe how the device is used in the novel and determine the author's purpose for using it.

Activity: "Language Locator"   **Page #:** 98-99   **Learning Type:** Individual/Collaborative
Description: Learn about seven types of figurative language and then find an example of each in the novel. Trade papers with partners and conduct scavenger hunts for such types of language as metaphor, idiom, and hyperbole.

Activity: "Section Log-In"   **Page #:** 100   **Learning Type:** Individual
Description: Choose from several options to add to Interactive Novel Logs.

A QUICK GUIDE TO . . .

+ +

Craft → the elements and devices an author uses to shape and create a unique story

+ +

Elements in Action → from *Because of Winn-Dixie* by Kate DiCamillo

Here are a few of the elements and literary devices Kate DiCamillo uses in her award-winning novel *Because of Winn-Dixie*:

Voice
The book is narrated by a smart, sassy 10-year-old girl named Opal.

Metaphor
Opal thinks of her father as a turtle hiding in his shell. The turtle shell is a metaphor for the way her father keeps his thoughts and feelings to himself and tries to protect himself from the outside world.

Foreshadowing
Midway through the novel, a thunderstorm scares Winn-Dixie so badly that he runs around crazily. Opal's father comments that they will need to look after Winn-Dixie any time a storm hits. Later in the novel, a bad thunderstorm strikes, but everyone is distracted and Winn-Dixie runs away.

Author's Craft

Symbolism
In Gloria Dump's backyard is a tree that has a bunch of bottles tied to its branches. Gloria says that each bottle represents something she has done wrong in the past.

Cliffhanger
While Winn-Dixie is gone, Opal worries that she has lost him forever. As readers, we don't know if that is what will happen or not.

Spotlight On → **Tone vs. Mood**

Related Ideas: author, reader, attitude, opinion, feelings, emotions

When we talk about literature, the terms *tone* and *mood* are similar. However, there are important differences between the two.

✦ Does the author reveal his or her attitudes or opinions toward the subject(s) about which he or she is writing? If so, these attitudes or opinions are referred to as the novel's **tone**.

✦ Does the novel cause its readers to experience certain emotions or feelings? If so, these emotions and feelings are referred to as the novel's **mood**.

THE LONG AND SHORT OF IT

Good writers know how to create rhythm and flow from language. The words they use are important, but so is the way they arrange those words into larger parts such as sentences, paragraphs, and chapters.

+ +

Chapters or page numbers in section: _____

+ +

1. Imagine if every sentence or every paragraph were the same length. How do you think that would affect the rhythm or flow of the story?

    _____

    _____

2. Now think about the chapters (or main parts) of the novel you are reading. Are some very short, while others are fairly long? Or are they mostly the same length?

    _____

    _____

3. If possible, choose one of each — a short chapter and a long one — and explain why each had to be the length it was.

    Name/Number of Chapter: _____ This chapter is short.

    The reason for this is _____

    _____

    _____

    Name/Number of Chapter: _____ This chapter is long.

    The reason for this is _____

    _____

    _____

4. What effect did reading chapters of different lengths have on you as a reader? How did it help/hurt your enjoyment of the novel?

    _____

    _____

    _____

    _____

NAME: _____

FORM FLIP

Literature can be written in a variety of forms, such as prose, poetry, or drama.

✦ **Prose** uses sentence and paragraphs to express ideas. This style of writing can sound similar to the way we speak.

✦ **Poetry** uses creative line breaks, stanzas, and vivid language to express feeling, emotions, and images in fewer words than prose. Some poems rhyme, though free-verse poetry does not.

✦ **Drama** is made up of two main components: dialogue and stage directions. Drama is often performed on a stage.

✦ ✦

Title of the Novel: _____

In which form is this novel written? _____

How do you know this? What elements does it contain that reveal its form? _____

_____

Think of an important scene or passage from the novel. Imagine if it were written in a different form. Imagine if, instead of the everyday language of prose, it were written in the vivid imagery of poetry or if every thought were spoken as in drama. Or, if it is written in poetry or drama, imagine how different the novel would be if it were written in prose. On the lines below, write the scene or passage in a different form. If you need more space, use the back of this paper.

_____

_____

_____

_____

_____

_____

_____

_____

How would the entire novel be affected if it were written in a different form? In your opinion, what would change the novel for the worse? Would anything be better about the novel?

_____

_____

_____

84

NAME: _____

BEGINNINGS AND ENDINGS

Most novels are divided into chapters or into some other parts. When a chapter or other part ends, it creates a short break in the story. Think about how the author of the novel you are reading did this, and then think of why the author chose to add these breaks in the story.

+ +

Chapters or page numbers in section: _____

+ +

The Beginnings

Each chapter or part begins with a sentence that the author hopes will make the reader want to read further. Choose a beginning of one of the chapters. Quote the sentence and then list the thoughts this one sentence puts into the mind of the reader. (For example, "What will happen next?" "How will this be resolved?" "How will the character react to that?"). Finally, explain why this opening sentence was effective in making you want to read deeper into the chapter.

Quote: _____

_____

Questions and Thoughts: _____

_____

_____

Why the Sentence Is Effective: _____

_____

The Endings

Each chapter or part ends with a sentence that the author hopes will make the reader want to flip to the next chapter and continue reading. Choose an ending of one of the chapters. Quote the sentence and then list the thoughts this one sentence puts into the mind of the reader. Finally, explain why this ending sentence was effective in making you want to immediately read the next chapter or part.

Quote: _____

_____

Questions and Thoughts: _____

_____

_____

Why the Sentence Is Effective: _____

_____

NAME: _____

EXPLICIT VS. IMPLICIT

Texts can have both an explicit meaning and an implicit meaning.

Explicit	Implicit
The words mean what they actually say. *Also called:* **literal**	The information is not stated, but we can use our previous knowledge and clues in the text to **infer** (make a logical guess about) what is being said.

+ +

Your teacher will choose three quotations from the novel. Copy these quotations and decide their literal meanings, as well as any information you can infer from them.

Quotation #1: _____

_____ Page number(s): _____

Explicit meaning: _____

What is not stated but can be inferred? _____

_____

How do you know this? _____

_____

Quotation #2: _____

_____ Page number(s): _____

Explicit meaning: _____

What is not stated but can be inferred? _____

_____

How do you know this? _____

_____

Quotation #3: _____

_____ Page number(s): _____

Explicit meaning: _____

What is not stated but can be inferred? _____

_____

How do you know this? _____

_____

NAME: _____

MEANINGS TO THE ENDS

In literature, the last lines — of chapters or scenes or of the novel itself — often hint at information. They often form questions that are not answered explicitly. Instead, the reader must infer the answers.

Write down the last lines to three chapters. For each, explain what has just happened leading up to that line. Then write the implication of that line. In other words, what information can the reader guess or assume from this one line?

Chapter: _____ Last Line: _____

_____

What has just happened? _____

What is the implication? _____

_____

Chapter: _____ Last Line: _____

_____

What has just happened? _____

What is the implication? _____

_____

Chapter: _____ Last Line: _____

_____

What has just happened? _____

What is the implication? _____

_____

Now find a last line of a chapter or scene that ends with explicit information — in other words, the author tells you exactly what is happening.

Chapter: _____ Last Line: _____

_____

Why do you think the author gives this information in this way to end this chapter or scene?

_____

_____

NAME: _____

PAINTING A PICTURE

In literature, the term *imagery* is used to describe language that gives a visual description of a scene. An author uses imagery to help readers form a picture of the place in which the scene takes place. Clear and vivid imagery also helps readers accurately picture the characters' actions and reactions.

Choose a scene that you feel is filled with vivid imagery. List some of the most descriptive words and phrases the author uses to create that imagery. For each word or phrase, check the box next to **setting** (where the scene takes place), **action** (what a character physically does), or **reaction** (how a character shows feeling).

Briefly describe the scene: _____

_____

_____

_____

_____

Word or Phrase	What It Shows	How It Paints a Picture for the Reader
	☐ setting ☐ action ☐ reaction	
	☐ setting ☐ action ☐ reaction	
	☐ setting ☐ action ☐ reaction	
	☐ setting ☐ action ☐ reaction	

88

NAME(S): _____

DESCRIPTIVE DISCUSSION

In the previous activity, you examined a scene and the imagery the author used to describe the setting and the characters within that scene. For this activity, work with a partner to discuss your findings. Begin by deciding which partner will speak first.

Speaker #1: _____ **Speaker #2:** _____

Speaker #1
✦ Tell your partner which scene you have chosen and describe it.
✦ Explain to your partner how the author's descriptions of the setting add to the mood of the scene or to your understanding of this scene.

Speaker #2
✦ Listen to your partner's words. Paraphrase them in the space below.

_____
_____
_____
_____
_____

✦ Tell your partner if you have anything to add or if you disagree with any of his/her ideas.

Now switch roles.

Speaker #2
✦ Tell your partner which scene you have chosen and describe it.
✦ Explain to your partner how the descriptions of a character's movements and expressions add to your chosen scene and to your understanding of the character.

Speaker #1
✦ Listen to your partner's words. Paraphrase them in the space below.

_____
_____
_____
_____
_____

✦ Tell your partner if you have anything to add or if you disagree with any of his/her ideas.

NAME(S): _____

TONE VS. MOOD

When we talk about literature, the terms *tone* and *mood* are similar. However, there are important differences between the two.

✦ A novel's **tone** is the author's attitude toward the subject about which he or she is writing.

✦ A novel's **mood** is the feeling and emotions it gives to the reader.

✦ +

Begin by checking <u>all</u> of the answers you believe correctly answer this question: *What would you say is the <u>tone</u> of the novel?*

☐ harsh ☐ light ☐ sly ☐ passionate ☐ ironic

☐ gentle ☐ heavy ☐ angry ☐ relaxed ☐ straightforward

Decide who will be Partner #1 and who will be Partner #2. Follow the instructions below to have a discussion about the tone and mood of the novel.

Partner #1: _____ **Partner #2:** _____

First	Take turns explaining your choices with your partner. Each partner should reveal two answers and use examples from this section to explain those choices.
Next	Partner #1 should answer this question aloud: *How are the tone and mood similar?* Partner #2 should listen to Partner #1's answer and repeat it aloud to his or her partner.
Then	Partner #2 should answer this question aloud: *How are the tone and mood different?* Partner #1 should listen to Partner #2's answer and repeat it aloud to his or her partner.
Finally	Work together to answer this question: *Are the tone and the mood more similar or different? In other words, does the author's feeling about the characters, events, and settings of the novel seem to be more similar or different to the emotions you feel as you read the novel?* Write your answers on the lines below.

_____

_____

_____

_____

_____

_____

_____

MAKING THE MOOD

Authors have many ways of creating a feeling or mood. Think about a scene from the novel that was filled with mood. Choose a scene that made you feel an emotion such as fear, anxiety, joy, excitement, anger, or dread.

Scene (the events that happen): _____

_____

Mood (the main feeling conveyed): _____

Complete the chart below. The column on the left lists five elements the author combined to create this scene. For each element, explain how it contributed to the mood of the scene.

Element	How It Contributed to the Mood
Plot (the events that happen)	
Setting (the time when and place where the events happen)	
Characterization (the people and animals in the story)	
Voice (the tone of the narrator who is telling the story)	
Dialogue (the words spoken by the characters)	

In your opinion, which of these elements — plot, setting, characterization, voice, or dialogue — was the most important for creating the mood of the scene? Check the box next to your answer, and then explain your choice on the lines below.

☐ Plot   ☐ Setting   ☐ Characterization   ☐ Voice   ☐ Dialogue

_____

_____

_____

_____

NAME: _____

SO TO SPEAK

Dialogue is an important ingredient in most novels. *Dialogue* is the term we use to describe an exchange of speech between characters.

For this activity, choose two scenes that include the main character speaking with one other character. Compare these two scenes.

	Exchange #1	Exchange #2
1. Page number(s)		
2. Which two characters are speaking?		
3. What is the dialogue mostly about?		

Look back at your answer to #2. Circle the name of the character who speaks the most during this scene.

4. What do you think this scene says about the main character? (Think about the amount of talking he/she does, what is said, how he/she interacts with the other person.)		
5. What do you think this scene says about the person speaking with the main character?		

92

NAME(S): _____

SPEAKING OF DIALOGUE

In the previous activity, you completed a chart in which you looked at two scenes and how the main character speaks to and interacts with other characters in the novel.

Work with a partner to discuss your findings. Begin by deciding which partner will speak first.

Speaker #1: _____   **Speaker #2:** _____

Speaker #1

Think about scenes that include dialogue between the main character and one other character. Choose one of those scenes. Choose the one that you think is the best example of the main character's personality and how he or she interacts with other characters.

✦ Tell your partner which scene you have chosen and describe it.

✦ Explain to your partner how this scene is a great example of the main character's personality. Quote some of the main character's speech to support your claim.

Speaker #2

✦ Listen to your partner's words. Tell him or her if you agree or disagree with them. Explain your opinion.

✦ Add any information that you feel your partner left out. Or, if you feel that there was an even better scene that uses dialogue to reveal the main character's personality, describe that scene.

Now switch roles.

Speaker #2

Think about scenes that include dialogue between the main character and one other character. Choose one of those scenes. Choose the one that you think is the best example of how another character interacts with the main character or how that other character feels about the main character.

✦ Tell your partner which scene you have chosen and describe it.

✦ Explain to your partner how this scene is a great example of another character's feeling toward the main character. Quote some of the other character's speech to support your claim.

Speaker #1

✦ Listen to your partner's words. Tell him or her if you agree or disagree with them. Explain your opinion.

✦ Add any information that you feel your partner left out. Or, if you feel that there was an even better scene that uses dialogue to reveal another character's feelings toward the main character, describe that scene.

NAME: _____

OH, THE IRONY

Authors use many literary devices to add interest and depth to their writing. One such literary device is irony. Within the plot of a story, an event could be described as ironic if it leads to a result that is the opposite of what a character or reader expects.

As you are reading the novel, look for these three types of irony:

Situational Irony	Dramatic Irony	Verbal Irony
what happens is the opposite of what is expected or appropriate	the reader understands more about the story's events than a character does	a character says one thing but really means the opposite

Complete the chart below. Try to find one or more examples of each type of irony. List the page number(s) where you found each and explain why each is an example of irony.

Page(s)	Quotation Containing Irony	Type of Irony	Why It Is Ironic
		☐ Situational ☐ Dramatic ☐ Verbal	
		☐ Situational ☐ Dramatic ☐ Verbal	
		☐ Situational ☐ Dramatic ☐ Verbal	

Author's
Craft

MORE THAN MEETS THE EYE

Symbolism is another important literary device that authors use to transform their novels into something more meaningful. A symbol is a person, place, or thing that stands for something beyond itself. In other words, a symbol is what it is, but it's also something greater.

Example: The Statue of Liberty is an enormous copper statue of a woman holding a torch. That's what it literally is. Symbolically, however, it represents freedom and a chance for a new life. It gained this symbolic meaning because immigrants to the United States saw this statue as they entered the country, and it gave them hope that a better life awaited them.

+ +

With a partner, think about symbolism in the novel you are reading. Choose one person, one place, and one object that you feel function as symbols. Discuss how each does this. Make decisions as a team before completing the form below. Defend your choices for symbols.

Type	Name	Symbolic Meaning in Novel	Evidence That Shows This
person			
place			
object			

NAME: _____

LEFT IN SUSPENSE

In literature, a cliffhanger is an ending — usually to a chapter — that leaves many questions unanswered and puts the readers in a state of suspense. What will happen next? There's only one thing to do: keep reading to find out.

+ +

Chapters or page numbers in section: _____

+ +

Analyze the use of cliffhanger in the section of the novel you are reading. How does it work, and why is it an effective choice for an author to use?

1. How does the chapter or scene end? _____

   _____

   _____

   _____

   _____

2. Why is this a cliffhanger? What information does it leave the reader wanting to know?

   _____

   _____

   _____

3. Because the author withholds this information, what effect does that have on the reader?

   _____

   _____

   _____

4. How soon after the cliffhanger does the author give the reader this information — at the beginning of the next chapter, later in the novel, etc.?

   _____

   _____

5. How do you feel about the way the cliffhanger is resolved? Was the resolution satisfying? Why or why not?

   _____

   _____

   _____

96

NAME: _____

IN THE PAST, IN THE FUTURE

In the world of a novel's characters, the action usually takes place in just one time: the present. Even if a book is set 100 years ago, it is the present for the characters. They do not know they are in a novel! And unless the author tells you, you do not know what happened in these characters' pasts or what will happen in their futures.

Two ways in which an author can give you a glimpse into the past or show you what might happen in the future are through the use of flashbacks and foreshadowing.

Flashback	**Foreshadowing**
In literature, this is a device in which the author shows you a scene or event that took place before the action of the novel began.	In literature, this is a device in which the author gives the reader a hint about what might happen in the future of the novel or beyond the time period described in the novel.

✦ ✦

Choose one of these two literary devices. Complete the form below.

Title of novel: _____

Literary device: _____

Page number(s) in novel: _____

Describe how this device is used: _____

_____

_____

What do you think was the author's purpose for using this device? How does the use of this device further the plot or give us more insight into a character? Explain.

_____

_____

_____

_____

_____

_____

_____

_____

NAME: _____

LANGUAGE LOCATOR

AN AUTHOR'S TOOLS

Authors use many tools to create vivid descriptions, memorable moments, and quotable dialogue. A lot of those tools can be found in a toolbox marked "Figurative Language." So what is figurative language?

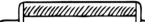

Figurative language uses words or expressions to imply (suggest) another meaning or to evoke (bring forth) an emotion.

Here is a list of several types of figurative language. Use this chart to help you complete the activity that follows.

Type	Meaning	Example(s)
alliteration	when a group of words uses the same sound to create an effect	*The wind whipped wildly across the wagon's wheels.*
hyperbole	a very dramatic exaggeration that can't literally be true	*I picked Jim to be on my team because he's 10 feet tall and faster than a cheetah.*
idiom	a phrase that has a figurative meaning that is very different from its literal meaning	*It was raining cats and dogs when I hit the hay. (It was pouring rain when I went to sleep.)*
metaphor	a statement that compares two things that are mostly not alike, usually by defining one thing as the other	*For the prisoner, freedom was a ship passing in the night.*
onomatopoeia	words that sound like the sounds they describe	*Buzz, zap, the fly flew into the electric trap.*
personification	when human characteristics or qualities are used to describe something that is not human	*The sun waved goodbye as it dipped below the horizon.*
simile	type of metaphor that uses the words "like" or "as" to compare two things that are mostly not alike	*Rick was as tired as an old shoe last night. He slept like a rock.*

LANGUAGE LOCATOR (CONT.)

SCAVENGER HUNT

Can you demonstrate your understanding of figurative language? Can you outsmart your classmates? Search the novel you are reading for examples of each type of figurative language listed below. When you find one, write down the page number on which the example is located. After you have located all seven, exchange papers with a classmate.

Use your partner's page numbers to locate all seven. For each, write down the quotation in which the figurative language is used. Leave the final column blank for now.

Type	Quotation	Meaning in Story
alliteration on page _____		
hyperbole on page _____		
idiom on page _____		
metaphor on page _____		
onomatopoeia on page _____		
personification on page _____		
simile on page _____		

After you have each found all seven, go back and discuss your findings. How does the author use figurative language in each example? What is the meaning of each in the story? Decide together and fill out the final column for each example.

SECTION LOG-IN

Use the prompts below to make a more personal connection to what you have read. Choose one of the following suggestions and use it to fill a page in your Interactive Novel Log. Take this opportunity to connect to the novel in a way that interests you.

Begin by reading each idea. Put a checkmark beside the ones that most appeal to you.

✦ ✦

Ideas for Your Interactive Novel Log

☐ **And I Quote** — As you read the novel, look for sentences (descriptions, dialogue, etc.) that stand out and are meaningful to you. Create a page of your favorite quotations from the book. Include page numbers.

☐ **Speaking of This Book** — Do you know someone who would love the style of this book? Write a dialogue between you and this person. Tell this person about the book and why you think he or she would love it. Try to use almost all dialogue as you write this scene.

☐ **Describe It** — Authors use imagery to describe both outdoor and indoor locations in their novels. Choose one outdoor place and one indoor place that you know well. Write paragraphs about these places. Use descriptive language to give the reader a sense of these places. Remember to appeal to the senses.

☐ **To Be Continued** — Think of the most exciting cliffhanger possible. What would make you want to read on to find out what happened to the hero of the story? Write your cliffhanger on a piece of paper. All papers should be mixed up by the teacher and redistributed. Use the cliffhanger you have been given to write the next paragraph in a book. For example, if the cliffhanger says the hero is falling out of a 10-story building, your paragraph could describe how the hero survives the fall and what he/she does next.

☐ **Back Before It Began** — Write a flashback scene that includes characters and/or settings from the novel. Your scene should show an event that happened in a time *before* the novel begins. If possible, your scene should hint at something that happens in the novel. In other words, include some foreshadowing in your flashback.

☐ **How I Felt** — How did this novel make you feel as you read it? Create a page of words, pictures, and colors that you feel describe the mood of the novel.

☐ **"Like" I Said** — Use similes to describe characters, settings, or events from the novel. You might even create a few similes to describe your experience of reading the novel. In all, form five similes and explain each.

☐ **Other** — Come up with an idea of your own! Your idea should be related to the concept of author's craft or to the specific craft or style of the novel you are reading.

_____

_____

TEACHER INSTRUCTIONS

An author chooses specific words in order to describe the world and convey the mood of a specific novel. A great novel's vocabulary is integral to its settings, characters, and themes. It is also an important part of any reading experience: students must understand the individual words in order to comprehend the meaning of the novel as a whole.

+ +

As your students read the novel, use the following worksheets to help them analyze and examine aspects related to vocabulary.

↩ *Activities marked with this icon are meant to be used after the reading of each section of the novel. At that time, distribute fresh copies of these pages. Completed copies should be included in each student's Interactive Novel Log.*

Activity: "My Word Wall" ↩ **Page #:** 102 **Learning Type:** Individual
Description: Identify unknown words while reading. Practice using context clues as well as reference materials to understand word meaning.

Activity: "Choice Words" ↩ **Page #:** 103 **Learning Type:** Individual
Description: In the novel, find a quotation in which the unknown word appears. Based on context, make a guess as to the word's meaning. Then look up the word and write its definition and part of speech. Use the word in a new sentence of your own creation.

Activity: "Alike and Opposite" ↩ **Page #:** 104 **Learning Type:** Individual
Description: Find a quotation in which the word appears. Identify its definition, part of speech, and connotation. List one synonym and one antonym of the word, rewrite the quotation with these words in place of the original word, and determine how the new word would affect the meaning of the quotation.
Teacher Tip: Use this activity with adjectives, action verbs, or other words that have natural synonyms and antonyms.

Activity: "Make the Case" **Page #:** 105 **Learning Type:** Individual
Description: Choose one noun, one verb, and one adjective that best describe the novel in some way. Support your choices with evidence from the text. Illustrate the word's usage in the novel.

Consider using the following activities to create even more learning experiences from the novel's vocabulary.

+ **Teach the teacher.** Assign a different word to each pair of students. Give groups time to research the word and its use in the novel. Have student pairs do short presentations on the word's meaning and use.

+ **Design an illustrated dictionary.** Choose several words from the novel. Draw pictures to depict those words.

+ **Write a poem.** Have students create poems that feature a set number of vocabulary words.

+ **Create a puzzle.** Have students choose a set number of vocabulary words and create puzzles from them. Students can create crossword puzzles, word searches, word ladders, anagrams, or any other type of puzzle they wish.

+ **Play a Jeopardy!-style game.** Make a game board with definitions of vocabulary words. Students compete to identify the correct words.

+ **Hold a vocabulary-in-context contest.** Have students write short stories that properly use as many vocabulary words as possible. Select a few stories with the highest number of vocabulary words used, read them aloud to the class, and have the class vote for the story that made the best use of vocabulary words.

NAME: _____

MY WORD WALL

Find your own vocabulary words. As you read the novel, look for words you don't know. Use this chart to write down the words and their meanings.

Word	Paragraph and Page Number	My Guess	Dictionary Definition	My Own Sentence

NAME: _____

CHOICE WORDS

+ +

Word from Novel: _____ **Page Number:** _____

+ +

1. Find one quotation in which this word appears in the novel. Write it in the box.

+---+
| |
| |
| |
| |
+---+

2. Reread the paragraph or section that contains the vocabulary word. Consider what is happening in the story and how the author uses the word. Based on the word and ideas around the word, what do you think it means? Explain.

_____

_____

_____

3. Now look up the word in the dictionary and write down the definition of this word that best fits the way it is used in the novel.

_____

_____

4. Does the word have other meanings that are different from the way it is used in the quotations? If so, list those meanings.

_____

_____

5. What is the part of speech of this word as it is used in the novel?

_____

6. Write your own sentence that uses the vocabulary word.

_____

_____

_____

7. When you think of this word and how it is used in the novel, what images does it bring to your mind? On the back of this paper, draw a picture to illustrate the word's meaning.

NAME: _____

ALIKE AND OPPOSITE

+ +

Word from Novel: _____ **Page Number:** _____

+ +

1. Find one quotation in which this word appears in the novel. Write it in the box.

   [   ]

2. What is the part of speech of this word as it is used in the quotation?

   ☐ noun   ☐ verb   ☐ adjective   ☐ adverb   ☐ other

3. What is the definition of the word as it is used in the quotation?

   _____

   _____

4. What is the connotation of the word as it is used in the quotation? Put a checkmark next to one of the following and explain your choice on the lines below.

   ☐ positive   ☐ negative   ☐ neutral (neither positive nor negative)

   _____

   _____

5. Think about words that have either the same meaning (synonyms) or the opposite meaning (antonyms) of the vocabulary word. Complete the chart. In the "Rewrite Quote" column, rewrite the quotation from the novel but replace the vocabulary word with either a synonym or antonym. Determine the effect this has on the meaning of the quotation.

	Word	Rewrite Quote	Is Meaning Changed?	How?
Synonym			☐ yes ☐ no	
Antonym			☐ yes ☐ no	

NAME: _____

MAKE THE CASE

Choose three words — one noun, one verb, and one adjective — that best describe and/or best represent this novel.

The Rules

1. Each word must be in the novel.
2. No proper nouns or proper adjectives allowed.
3. In the "Why You Chose This Word" column, give reasons from the text to defend each choice. Use complete sentences to list your reasons.
4. In the "Draw a Picture" column, illustrate how the word is used in the novel.

+ +

Descriptive Word	Why You Chose This Word	Draw a Picture
noun		
verb		
adjective		

TEACHER INSTRUCTIONS

After your students have finished reading the novel, they can further their in-depth analyses of the novel through the use of the following worksheets:

Activity: "Sum It All Up"　　　**Page #:** 108–109　　　**Learning Type:** Individual/Collaborative
Description: Use the skills practiced in each section in order to summarize the novel as a whole. Explain and expand on summarization choices. Then, use the "Peer Review" worksheet to analyze a classmate's summary.

Activity: "A Novel Encyclopedia"　　　**Page #:** 110–111　　　**Learning Type:** Individual/Collaborative
Description: Create an encyclopedia page for one aspect (character, setting, theme, etc.) of the novel. Examine this one element closely in order to write about its background and to describe how it functions in the novel.
Teacher Tip: Follow the instructions given on page 110 to create a class encyclopedia of the novel.

Activity: "A Novel Poster"　　　**Page #:** 112–113　　　**Learning Type:** Collaborative
Description: Collaborate to create a poster that identifies key points in a chapter and shows understanding of the elements that contribute to that chapter's success.
Teacher Tip: Follow the detailed teacher instructions provided on page 112.

Activity: "Interview a Character"　　　**Page #:** 114　　　**Learning Type:** Collaborative
Description: In pairs, role-play as a character and an interviewer in front of the class. Utilize the tips provided at the bottom of the page in order to bring a secondary character to life.

Activity: "Connect the Plots"　　　**Page #:** 115　　　**Learning Type:** Collaborative
Description: In front of the class, demonstrate connections between the people, places, and things that populate the novel.
Teacher Tip: This teacher page gives detailed instructions for setting up the student activity.

Activity: "An Elemental Choice"　　　**Page #:** 116　　　**Learning Type:** Individual
Description: Plan and write a persuasive essay on which element most makes the novel special: voice, plot, or theme.
Teacher Tip: Distribute the "Checking It Twice" worksheet (page 117) and have students do both self reviews and peer reviews of their work.

Activity: "Checking It Twice"　　　**Page #:** 117　　　**Learning Type:** Individual/Collaborative
Description: After drafting persuasive essays, use the first checklist to self-assess your rough draft. Then exchange papers with one or more students and complete the "Peer Review" questionnaire. Use this input to revise writing and create a final draft.

Activity: "Writing a Persuasive Letter"　　　**Page #:** 118–119　　　**Learning Type:** Individual
Description: Using a letter format, write an essay that gives an opinion, considers opposing views, introduces reasons, and provides evidence from the text.
Teacher Tip: Distribute the "Checking It Twice" worksheet (page 117) and have students do both self reviews and peer reviews of their work.

TEACHER INSTRUCTIONS (CONT.)

Activity: "From Page to Screen"   **Page #:** 120   **Learning Type:** Individual
Description: Compare and contrast the filmed version to the novel. Examine the experience of watching the film vs. reading the novel. Note changes the filmmakers made to the story and determine the effectiveness of these choices.
Teacher Tip: Use this activity for novels that have had been adapted as films. If possible, show the entire film to your students after they have read the novel. (Remember to view the film in its entirety beforehand to determine its appropriateness for your students.) You may also choose to show only a few representative scenes that will give students an idea of the choices the filmmakers made when casting and adapting the novel.

Activity: "Pitch the Sequel"   **Page #:** 121   **Learning Type:** Individual
Description: Write a proposal for a sequel to the novel. Determine which elements (characters, settings, events) will be included and why this sequel would honor the original and be an exciting addition to it.

Activity: "Acting Out"   **Page #:** 122–123   **Learning Type:** Collaborative
Description: Work within a large group to dramatize a scene from the novel. Describe the events that will be dramatized. List the characters, props, and dialogue that are integral to the scene.
Teacher Tip: Divide the class into groups of 4–6 students. Offer ideas for scenes that can be dramatized. Consider suggesting scenes that must have taken place but aren't specifically written in the novel. For example, if the novel is narrated from a limited perspective (first-person or third-person limited), there are scenes that the narrator – and thus, the reader – does not witness. Have students use their knowledge of the novel and its characters to guess what exactly took place during those scenes.

Activity: "Create a Book Trailer"   **Page #:** 124–125   **Learning Type:** Individual/Collaborative
Description: Learn about book trailers and brainstorm ideas about creative trailers for the novel. Use the first page of the activity to plan and the second page to sketch images for the novel's trailer. Explain what these images would reveal about the novel.
Teacher Tip: Consider allowing students to use movie-making software to create actual trailers based on their sketches. This project can be done individually or collaboratively.

Activity: "My Book Rating"   **Page #:** 126   **Learning Type:** Individual
Description: Use a rating system to evaluate different components of the story before making a final evaluation of the book as a whole.

Here's Another Idea: Historiated Initials

Have your students create **historiated intials** for the novel they are reading. A historiated initial is an ornate, oversized letter at the beginning of a paragraph or other section of text. In and around this letter are drawings that depict identifiable images from the novel. (See the example to the right.)

+ To begin, use a search engine to locate appropriate example of historiated initials that will give your students an understanding of the concept.

+ Next, have students locate a line of text that they wish to illustrate.

+ Give students the necessary time and materials to devise and revise their rewriting of this line with a historiated initial.

+ Display student work and/or conduct collaborative discussions on students' line choices and illustrations.

NAME: _____

SUM IT ALL UP

Now that you have finished the novel — and have had a lot of practice with summarization — use your skills to write a very brief summary of the entire novel. Fit your summary on the lines below. To do so, you must include only the most important events in your summary.

_____

_____

_____

_____

_____

_____

_____

_____

_____

_____

_____

_____

_____

After you have completed your summary, answer the following questions.

1. If you could have included information about one more event or character in the novel, what (or whom) would you have written about? Why?

_____

_____

_____

_____

2. Would you say that this book is easy or challenging to summarize? Explain.

_____

_____

_____

_____

Exchange papers with another student. Complete the "Peer Review" activity on the following page.

NAME: _____

SUM IT ALL UP (CONT.)

Read a classmate's summary of the novel. Respond to the questions below.

PEER REVIEW

Your Name: _____

Writer's Name: _____

Name of Novel: _____

Check the **Yes** or **No** box for each statement.   **Yes**   **No**

- The summary focuses on only the novel's most important points.   ☐   ☐

- The summary includes the name(s) of the novel's most important character(s).   ☐   ☐

- The writer uses his or her own words to describe the novel's plot.   ☐   ☐

- Transition words are used to show the sequence in which events occur in the novel.   ☐   ☐

- The summary is free of spelling or grammar errors.   ☐   ☐

What was the best thing about this summary? Explain your answer.

_____

_____

_____

_____

_____

Would this summary give someone who hasn't read the novel a good idea of what the novel is about? Why or why not?

_____

_____

_____

_____

_____

_____

_____

A NOVEL ENCYCLOPEDIA

TEACHER INSTRUCTIONS

For this activity, your students will be combining their knowledge of the novel they are reading in order to create a comprehensive Wikipedia-style class encyclopedia about it.

Preparation

Compile a list of elements from the novel so that you have one element per student in your class. Consider the following elements from the novel:

- ✦ **Characters** (protagonist, antagonist, supporting characters, narrator)

- ✦ **Objects** (important objects that carry symbolic value, are the cause of major events, are the result of major events, etc.)

- ✦ **Settings** (places where action occurs in the story)

- ✦ **Events** (major happenings that take place in the novel or before the novel begins but have an important effect on the story of the novel)

If you wish to assign these elements by choosing them out of a hat, then prepare a paper label for each element. Or, you may wish to use an online list randomizer to assign elements to students.

Assignment Directions

1. Assign a unique element to each student. Distribute an encyclopedia page template (page 111) to each student.

2. As a class, decide on the name of your encyclopedia and have each student fill out the top of their papers.

3. Give each student time to fill out the rest of their forms. For each element, students will provide the following information from the novel:

   - ✦ **Overview:** This is a very brief summary of the element (character, setting, etc.).

   - ✦ **Background:** In this section, students should supply a little history of the character, setting, etc., from *before* the novel begins. In other words, "What can be said about this element before the story began?"

   - ✦ **Role in the Novel:** Here, students should detail what happens to the element *during* the novel.

4. When individual students have completed their pages, conduct a peer or class review of each page. Was any important information left out? Was any erroneous information included? Give entries back to those who wrote them, along with a clean copy of the template. Allow students time to rewrite their entries, with the necessary changes made.

5. Collect the final drafts of students' entries and compile them into a class encyclopedia about the novel you are reading.

A NOVEL ENCYCLOPEDIA

ENTRY TEMPLATE

_____

(name of encyclopedia)

an encyclopedia devoted to _____

(name of novel)

+ + + + + + + + + + + + + + + + + + + +

_____

(name of element from the novel)

Overview

Background

Role in the Novel

A NOVEL POSTER

TEACHER INSTRUCTIONS

This activity offers students an opportunity to demonstrate understanding of the novel by creating visual representations of its parts.

Materials Required: poster board, markers

Optional Materials: scissors, glue, magazines, Internet access, sticky notes

✦ To begin, divide the class into groups of students. The ideal number in each group is 3 or 6, but smaller or larger groups will also be possible.

✦ Next, assign one chapter or section from the novel to each group.

✦ Distribute the second page of this activity (page 113), one per group. Each group will create a poster based on its assigned chapter or section. Have students read the instructions for what to include on their posters.

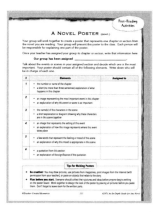

✦ Give students plenty of time to plan and create their posters. If you wish, allow them to access magazines or the Internet in search of appropriate images to include.

✦ After each group has completed its poster, hang the posters around the room. Conduct a gallery walk.

Ideas for a Gallery Walk

Allow students to move around the room and examine each poster. Equip students with sticky notes. When they have questions regarding another group's poster, they can write their questions on sticky notes and attach these notes directly to the poster. Guide your students to think about the following ideas as they prepare to ask questions:

✓ Is an idea on the poster not clear?

✓ Do you disagree with a point the poster makes?

✓ Do you want more information about something the group has included?

✓ Do you want to ask how the group felt about any particular scene or character?

✓ Do you want to bring up something you thought was important in that chapter but isn't included on the poster?

Once students have completed this process, allow groups to answer the questions attached to their posters.

A NOVEL POSTER (CONT.)

Your group will work together to create a poster that represents one chapter or section from the novel you are reading. Your group will present this poster to the class. Each person will be responsible for explaining one part of the poster.

Once your teacher has assigned your group its chapter or section, write that information here:

Our group has been assigned _____.

Talk about the events or scenes in your assigned section and decide which one is the most important. Your poster should contain all of the following elements. Write down who will be in charge of each one.

#	Elements	Assigned to
1	• the number or name of the chapter • a short (no more than three sentences) explanation of what happens in this chapter	
2	• an image representing the most important event in this chapter • an explanation of why this event or scene is so important	
3	• the name(s) of the characters in the scene • a short explanation or diagram showing why these characters are in this scene together	
4	• an image that represents the setting of this event • an explanation of how this image represents where this event takes place	
5	• a few words that represent the feeling or mood of this scene • an explanation of why this mood is appropriate in this scene	
6	• a quotation from this section • an explanation of the significance of the quotation	

Tips for Making Posters

✦ **Be creative!** You may draw pictures, use pictures from magazines, print images from the Internet (with permission from your teacher), or paste on objects that relate to the story.

✦ **Plan before you start.** Everyone should collect their pictures and ideas before anyone begins writing on the poster board. Work together to design the look of the poster by placing all pictures before you paste them. Don't forget to leave room for the written parts.

NAME(S): _____

INTERVIEW A CHARACTER

Most novels have one main character, but the other characters are important, too. The secondary characters help readers understand the main character better and help move the plot along. You and a partner will analyze one secondary character and create a mock interview that demonstrates the character's personality.

Your teacher will assign one of these secondary characters to you and your partner. Once you have been assigned a character, write his or her name here:

You and your partner will present a live interview that features your assigned character. One of you will pretend to be the character, while the other will be the interviewer. Work together to plan your interview. Write six questions you would like to ask your assigned character. Use questions that require more than a one-word answer. In order to do this, use question starters such as the following:

1. Tell us about _____

2. What did you think when _____

3. How would you _____

4. Explain why _____

Now come up with two questions of your own.

5. _____

_____

6. _____

_____

Interviewer Tips	Interviewee Tips
☐ Before the actual presentation, prepare note cards with brief hints that will help you.	☐ Pretend that you are the character throughout the interview.
☐ Begin by giving the audience a brief introduction to the character.	☐ Answer the questions the way you think the character would.
☐ Listen to the interviewee's responses and wait until your partner is finished speaking before moving on to the next question.	☐ Try to talk and act the way the character would.
☐ After your questions, ask the audience if they have any questions for the character.	☐ Listen to the interviewer carefully. Wait until he or she is finished asking each question before responding.

CONNECT THE PLOTS

TEACHER INSTRUCTIONS

Most novels contain a large number of characters, settings, and important objects. Use this activity to illustrate the connectedness of the people, places, and things in the novel.

1. **Create a bulletin board of labels.**
   On fairly large labels or pieces of construction paper, write the names of the people, places, and things that populate the novel. Then set up a display. You may use pushpins to attach the labels on a bulletin board, or you can affix magnets to the backs of the labels and place them on a whiteboard. A third option would be to write the labels on a chalkboard. In all instances, the labels should be placed/written in a random order on the board. The labels should be spread out, with plenty of space between them.

2. **Randomly announce two people, places, and/or things from the labels.**
   Place a second set of labels in a hat or other container. Pull out two labels and read each aloud. Students will be asked to explain how two people, places, and/or things in the novel are connected. Some combinations of people, places, and things will have obvious connections. Others will require a few intermediate connections to be made first.

3. **Explain to students how they will be illustrating the connection between these two people, places, and/or things.**
   If using pushpins on a bulletin board, give students string or yarn. Have them hook the yarn onto the pushpin affixed to the first label. Then have them pull the yarn over to the next label if there is a direct connection. If there is not, students must pull the yarn to a direct connection and continue to do this until they make a connection with the second label chosen by you. If a whiteboard/chalkboard is used, follow the same logic as detailed above by having students use whiteboard pens/chalk to draw lines between the connections.

4. **Choose a student to illustrate the connection between these two people, places, and/or things.**
   Allow students to demonstrate speaking skills as they explain these connections. For most combinations of objects, students will need to make intermediate connections in order to connect the two original items. As a student makes each connection, he or she will explain the connection aloud to the class.

   Example from *Holes*: If the two labels chosen are "Myra Menke" and "Onions," a student might say the following while demonstrating the connection at the board:

   "Myra Menke" was the love interest of "Elya Yelnats" who was the father of "Stanley Yelnats I" who survived for 17 days in the mountains near "God's Thumb," which is where "Onions" have grown for over a century.

5. **Allow discussion.**
   Give students an opportunity to agree or disagree with the speaker. Also allow them to offer other ways of connecting the two people, places, or things.

6. **Repeat this process until each student has had a chance to demonstrate a connection on the board.**

NAME: _____

AN ELEMENTAL CHOICE

In literature, three of the terms that we can discuss are **voice**, **plot**, and **theme**.

Voice	**Plot**	**Theme**
the speech and thought patterns of the first-person narrator	the events that take place in the novel	the underlying idea(s) or message(s) in the novel

Your assignment is to write an essay in which you argue that one of these elements is the most important part of the novel. Do you think that what makes this novel the most special is the voice of its narrator, the events that happen, or the ideas about life that the author has included?

+ +

Follow this outline in writing your essay. Use the space provided to brainstorm ideas and to plan your rough draft.

Paragraph 1: Set up your essay by introducing the three terms and giving a brief description of the how each element is used in the novel.

How **Voice** is used: _____

_____

How **Plot** is used: _____

_____

How **Theme** is used: _____

_____

Finish this first paragraph by stating which element you feel most makes the novel unique, interesting, or entertaining.

Paragraph 2: Use this paragraph to support the claim you made at the end of Paragraph 1. Provide three examples that show how this element contributes to the success of the novel.

Example 1: _____

Example 2: _____

Example 3: _____

Paragraph 3: Restate your opinion and wrap up your essay.

After you have completed this outline, write a rough draft of your essay on a separate piece of paper.

CHECKING IT TWICE

SELF-EDITING CHECKLIST

After writing your rough draft, use this checklist to make sure your essay has everything that is required. Check off the box next to each item once you have included that element in your essay.

- ☐ My introduction states my topic and the point I will make about it.

- ☐ I have used at least one quotation or example in each body paragraph.

- ☐ I included page numbers of quotations from the novels.

- ☐ I have explained all quotations and examples.

- ☐ My conclusion wraps up my essay well.

- ☐ Throughout my essay, I used transition words to show how one idea relates to the next.

- ☐ I have reread my essay to check for spelling, punctuation, and sentence mistakes.

One thing I need help with is

PEER-EDITING CHECKLIST

Have your partner read your essay, check a box for each statement, and respond to the questions below.

Reader's Name: _____	Yes	No
• The introduction does a good job explaining the point the writer will make.	☐	☐
• There are quotations or examples in every body paragraph.	☐	☐
• Each quotation and example clearly supports the paragraph's point.	☐	☐

The paragraph that does this best is _____.

A paragraph that is confusing, unclear, or not detailed is _____.

| • The conclusion wraps up the essay well. | ☐ | ☐ |

(Circle one.) There are   **no   some   many**   spelling errors or sentence mistakes.

Suggestions: _____

_____

_____

NAME: _____

WRITING A PERSUASIVE LETTER

Imagine a school in another town is considering using this novel in their classrooms. They want to find out what students who have read the book think about it. Write a letter to the school board explaining why you would or would not recommend this novel for their school. In your argument, include two reasons why you do or do not recommend the book. Also identify one opposing or alternate view. Explain why you disagree with this view, or explain why your reasons are stronger.

✦ ✦

Plan Your Argument

Before you begin, brainstorm ideas. Try to think of as many points as you can for both sides. Try to think about what reasons other people might give, even if you do not agree with them. Think about the writing style, characters, plot, theme, point of view, or any other writing-related topic.

Reasons to Recommend	Reasons to Not Recommend

(Check one.) My essay will ☐ **recommend** ☐ **not recommend** the novel.

Which two reasons will you use to support your opinion? Select the two strongest points from your brainstorming list. For each reason, provide evidence in the form of an example or quotation from the novel.

Reason 1: _____

_____

Evidence: _____

_____

Reason 2: _____

_____

Evidence: _____

WRITING A PERSUASIVE LETTER (CONT.)

Look at the brainstorming list for the opposite side of your argument. Pick one reason from that list to explain and argue against.

Opposing viewpoint: _____

Evidence: _____

My reaction: _____

✦ ✦

Create an Outline

Follow this outline and write your letter on a separate piece of paper. Remember to begin your letter with a greeting and end it with your name and signature.

Paragraph 1: Introduction

✦ Explain your experience with the book. (Why did you read it? What did you think as you read it?)

✦ Write your thesis statement, using this formula:

Although **[opposing point]**, I **[do/do not]** recommend *[name of novel]* because **[reason 1]** and **[reason 2]**.

Paragraph 2: Explain your first reason.

✦ Give one example or quotation from the book that demonstrates your point.

✦ Explain how that example or quotation proves your point.

Paragraph 3: Explain your second reason.

✦ Give another example or quotation from the book that demonstrates your point.

✦ Explain how that example or quotation proves your point.

Paragraph 4: Acknowledge the opposing view.

✦ Explain why you disagree with this point *or* why your reasons are more important.

✦ Give one example or quotation from the book that demonstrates your point.

Paragraph 5: Conclude your letter.

✦ Explain how you think the students will respond to this book. Focus on the way it will make them feel or think about the situation described in the novel.

✦ Write a concluding sentence that restates your recommendation.

NAME: _____

FROM PAGE TO SCREEN

Books and movies just naturally seem to go together. Most authors try to create vivid imagery that helps their readers picture the characters, settings, and events in their novels. It's only natural that many who read the story on the page want to see it on a screen.

Answer the following questions about the film adaptation of the novel you are reading.

+ +

Title of the Novel: _____

1. Before you watched the film, what were you most excited or interested to see? Name a character, setting, or scene from the novel. Explain why you wanted to see this on the screen.

   _____

   _____

   Once you watched the film, were you pleased or disappointed with how this character, setting, or scene is portrayed in the film? Explain your answer.

   _____

   _____

2. How is the film different from the movie? Were any major changes made? Were any scenes or characters added or subtracted?

   _____

   _____

   Why do you think the film's writer(s) and director(s) made these choices? Why do you think they added or subtracted certain scenes, characters, etc.?

   _____

   _____

3. Write about the actors who portrayed — or voiced, if the film is animated — the characters. Which actors were perfect for their roles? In your opinion, were any not so good? Why?

   _____

   _____

4. Did the film change or alter your opinion of the book in any way? For example, did seeing the film make anything in the book clearer or more enjoyable?

   _____

   _____

5. In your opinion, which was better: the novel or the film? On the back of this paper, give your answer and explain your reasons for feeling this way.

PITCH THE SEQUEL

Once you finish reading the final page of the novel, the story is over and nothing else can be known about what happens to the people, places, and things that populate the novel. But it doesn't have to be this way! Books and movies often have sequels — stories that are set in the same world as the original but describe events that take place afterward.

Imagine you have been asked to write a proposal for a sequel to the novel you have just read. Fill out the form below to give your best ideas about what a sequel for this novel would include.

The Sequel to _____
(title of novel)

Plot summary of the sequel (what happens): _____

_____

_____

_____

_____

_____

_____

_____

Characters in sequel:

From original novel: _____

_____

Newly created for the sequel: _____

_____

Main conflict in the sequel (what causes trouble for the main character): _____

_____

_____

_____

Why readers of the original novel would find this sequel interesting: _____

_____

_____

_____

NAME(S): _____

ACTING OUT

Work with your group to dramatize a scene from the novel. It can be a scene that is written about in detail in the novel, or it can be one that must have taken place but that is not written about.

Once your group has chosen a scene, write the details of that scene here.

Summary of the Scene

With your group, you are going to write a script on a separate piece of paper. This script will show what the characters say and do.

✦ Follow the tips given below. They show you how to format your script.

✦ Use the second page of this activity to plan your scene. Who will play which role? What props will be needed? What lines of dialogue will be important to include?

Tips for Writing a Script

Your script should contain these three elements:

- **Character Names** — The name of the characters in the scene should be written in the script. *Each time a character's name appears, it should be written in uppercase letters. Each time the character speaks, his or her name should be centered over his or her words.*

- **Dialogue** — Dialogue is what the characters say. Most of your script will be dialogue. You do not need to put quotation marks around dialogue in your script. *Center each line of dialogue under the name of the character who is speaking.*

- **Stage Directions** — This information describes what the characters should be doing in the scene or other things that are happening besides dialogue. This information helps the actors know what to do. These sentences are not read or spoken out loud. Instead, the audience sees the actors perform these actions. *Put these sentences in parentheses.*

After your group has finished writing the script, practice the scene together. Then act out your scene for the class.

ACTING OUT (CONT.)

Cast (the characters in the scene)

Name all of the characters involved in the scene. Not all need to be portrayed if there are more characters than there are members in your group.

Who are the characters in this scene?	Who will play each character?

Props (the objects in the scene)

Prop Needed	Why?

Dialogue (the words spoken in the scene)

Important Line to Include	Why?

NAME: _____

CREATE A BOOK TRAILER

When was the last time you went to see a movie in a theater? Before the movie began, the theater most likely showed trailers for other films. What is a trailer?

> **Trailer**
>
> a series of images from or about a work of art (film, novel, etc.) presented with the purpose of increasing an audience's interest in that work

These days, many books have trailers that present a series of images designed to give an audience an idea of the contents and tone of the novel. Some trailers recreate a single scene from the novel, while others string together many moments from several scenes. Some show entirely new ideas and images that are related to the novel in some way.

What style would you use to create an effective trailer for the novel? Use the space below to brainstorm ideas. Then, complete the following page to sketch images that would fit in the trailer.

+ +

Name of the Novel: _____

What would you like a viewer of your trailer to feel about the novel?

_____

_____

_____

_____

_____

What types of images would convey this feeling? Why?

_____

_____

_____

_____

_____

_____

_____

_____

NAME: _____

CREATE A BOOK TRAILER (CONT.)

Draw six images that, when combined, would create a trailer for this novel. Below each image, tell what the image shows and explain why you chose to show that image.

1.	2.	3.
What it shows: _____ _____ _____ Why: _____ _____ _____	What it shows: _____ _____ _____ Why: _____ _____ _____	What it shows: _____ _____ _____ Why: _____ _____ _____
4.	**5.**	**6.**
What it shows: _____ _____ _____ Why: _____ _____ _____	What it shows: _____ _____ _____ Why: _____ _____ _____	What it shows: _____ _____ _____ Why: _____ _____ _____

NAME: _____

MY BOOK RATING

What did you like or dislike about the book? Think about the story elements and rank each one. Use the following rating scale.

0 stars	1 star	2 stars	3 stars	4 stars	5 stars
☆☆☆☆☆	★☆☆☆☆	★★☆☆☆	★★★☆☆	★★★★☆	★★★★★
terrible	bad	okay	good	great	amazing!

Characters ☆☆☆☆☆

Reason: _____

Setting ☆☆☆☆☆

Reason: _____

Point of View ☆☆☆☆☆

Reason: _____

Plot ☆☆☆☆☆

Reason: _____

The Ending ☆☆☆☆☆

Reason: _____

Theme ☆☆☆☆☆

Reason: _____

Overall, I give this book _____ stars because _____

_____

_____

TEACHER INSTRUCTIONS

Text sets offer a way to strengthen students' understanding of literature and examine the ways different authors approach similar material. After students have read two pieces of fiction that can be connected, compared, and contrasted, use the following activities.

Activity: "Character Comparisons"   **Page #:** 128   **Learning Type:** Collaborative
Description: List words that describe each protagonist, choose a common trait, and decide how this trait influences each character's behavior within the story.

Activity: "Trading Traits"   **Page #:** 129   **Learning Type:** Individual
Description: Choose a way in which the two protagonists are not alike, and decide how their novels would be different if they swapped these traits. **Teacher Tip:** This activity should be done after students complete "Character Comparisons."

Activity: "Discussing Changes"   **Page #:** 130   **Learning Type:** Collaborative
Description: Work with groups to track the changes in feelings the protagonists have from the beginnings of the novels to the ends.

Activity: "Thanks for the Support"   **Page #:** 131   **Learning Type:** Individual
Description: List the supporting characters from each story and decide which ones most influenced the main characters. Cite evidence to support claims.

Activity: "We Got Plot"   **Page #:** 132   **Learning Type:** Individual
Description: List and sequence the events that take place in each novel. Decide which novel contains more events and why.

Activity: "A Plot Alike and Different"   **Page #:** 133   **Learning Type:** Collaborative
Description: Look closely at the similarities and differences in the plots of the two stories. Decide on the genre of each story.
Teacher Tip: Review genre types with students, if necessary.

Activity: "Two Points of View"   **Page #:** 134   **Learning Type:** Individual
Description: Examine the narration used in each story. Determine the purpose for each narrative choice.

Activity: "Conflicting Answers"   **Page #:** 135   **Learning Type:** Collaborative
Description: Work in a group to look at how the protagonists of each story face four different types of conflict. Compare and contrast their experiences. **Teacher Tip:** Divide the class into groups of three or four, if possible.

Activity: "Get Settings, Go!"   **Page #:** 136   **Learning Type:** Collaborative
Description: Work with a partner to brainstorm lists of different locations in each book. Take turns explaining the importance of one location in each of the books.

Activity: "On Location"   **Page #:** 137   **Learning Type:** Individual
Description: Imagine that a character from one story is placed into the setting of another. Write a short scene in which that character adapts to the new surroundings. **Teacher Tip:** Remind students that setting refers to both place *and* time.

Activity: "Theme Seeds"   **Page #:** 138   **Learning Type:** Individual
Description: Compare and contrast how a common theme appears in each novel. Provide textual evidence to support answers.
Teacher Tip: Review "List of Common Themes" (page 74) in order to give students many ideas and choices.

Activity: "Section Log-In"   **Page #:** 139   **Learning Type:** Individual
Description: Choose from several options to add to Interactive Novel Logs.

NAME(S): _____

CHARACTER COMPARISONS

With a partner, brainstorm a list of traits that describe the protagonist of each story. Discuss which traits they have in common. Together, decide which trait is most important and why.

Words that describe   **Words that describe**

_____   **Words that** _____
(name of one main character)   **describe both**   *(name of other main character)*

1. Which one of these common traits do you and your partner think is the most important for both characters to have? Why?

_____

_____

2. How does this trait help each character? Give one example for each character.

Character: _____

How it helps: _____

Example: _____

Character: _____

How it helps: _____

Example: _____

TRADING TRAITS

In the previous activity, you looked closely at a trait that the two main characters have in common. Now consider how the two characters are most different.

One important way that _____ and _____ are not alike is

_____.

Cite an example from each story to show this difference.

Title: _____

Quotation or summary of scene: _____

_____

_____

_____

Title: _____

Quotation or summary of scene: _____

_____

_____

_____

Think about these two characters and the way in which they are not alike. How would they be different and how would the entire books be different if these two characters switched traits? Complete these thoughts.

If _____ were
         (main character)
_____, then
      (trait)
_____
      (title of novel)
would be different because _____

_____

_____

_____

_____.

If _____ were
         (main character)
_____, then
      (trait)
_____
      (title of novel)
would be different because _____

_____

_____

_____

_____.

NAME(S): _____

DISCUSSING CHANGES

In small groups, discuss how the main character of each novel felt at the **beginning** of his/her book. Use the chart below to jot down notes.

	Novel #1	Novel #2
Main Character		
Feelings About Self		
Feelings About Family		
Feelings About Peers		
Feelings About Society		

Now, discuss and take notes about how each main character felt at the **end** of his/her novel.

	Novel #1	Novel #2
Main Character		
Feelings About Self		
Feelings About Family		
Feelings About Peers		
Feelings About Society		

Discuss how these main characters changed by the end of the novels. As a group, answer the following questions. For each, write a short summary of your group's answer.

1. How did friendships/family help the two main characters change?

_____

_____

2. How did events/circumstances help the two main characters change?

_____

_____

130

NAME: _____

THANKS FOR THE SUPPORT

Think about the secondary or supporting characters in each story and how they influence the main characters. Begin by naming as many supporting characters from each novel as you can.

	Novel #1	Novel #2
Title		
Supporting Characters		

All of the characters you named are important in the stories. Which one from each story do you think was the most important in helping the protagonist to overcome the conflict and to grow and change?

In _____, the main character's name is
(title of Novel #1)
_____, and this character is most influenced by _____
(name of supporting character)

because _____

_____.

Here is a quotation that shows this: _____

_____

In _____, the main character's name is
(title of Novel #2)
_____, and this character is most influenced by _____
(name of supporting character)

because _____

_____.

Here is a quotation that shows this: _____

_____

Are the two supporting characters you picked more similar or different? Explain.

_____

_____

_____

NAME: _____

WE GOT PLOT

The plot is what happens in the story. It is all of the events that take place in the story. The sequence is the order in which the events of the plot take place.

Think about the sequence of the plot of each novel. For each section of each novel, make a list of three events that take place. Put those events in the order in which they occur in the novel.

	Novel #1	Novel #2
Title		
Beginning	1.	1.
	2.	2.
	3.	3.
Middle	1.	1.
	2.	2.
	3.	3.
End	1.	1.
	2.	2.
	3.	3.

Which novel has more events in its plot? _____

Explain why you think this is. _____

_____

_____

A PLOT ALIKE AND DIFFERENT

Think about the plots of each novel. Work with a partner to complete the following chart and answer the questions below.

Similarities in Plots	Differences in Plots

1. What is the most significant similarity? Why? _____

_____

_____

_____

2. What is the most significant difference? Why? _____

_____

_____

_____

✦ ✦

Considering Genre: Name the genre that you feel best describes each novel. Explain.

Novel #1 Title: _____ Genre: _____

Why? _____

_____

_____

Novel #2 Title: _____ Genre: _____

Why? _____

_____

_____

NAME: _____

TWO POINTS OF VIEW

Compare and contrast the points of view of the two stories you have read.

	Novel #1	**Novel #2**
Title		
Type of Narrator (check one)	☐ first-person Name: _____ ☐ third-person limited ☐ third-person omniscient	☐ first-person Name: _____ ☐ third-person limited ☐ third-person omniscient
Quotation That Shows Type of Narration		

If the novels have the <u>same</u> type of narration . . .	**If the novels have a <u>different</u> type of narration . . .**
1. How does this make the stories similar in how events are told to the reader? **2.** Even though they are the same type of narrator, how are these narrators different? Give examples.	**1.** Why do you think these authors chose to use different types of narration? How did each type serve each story? **2.** How do the different types of narration give you different insight into the lives of the main characters of these stories? Explain.

1. _____

   _____

   _____

   _____

2. _____

   _____

   _____

   _____

CONFLICTING ANSWERS

The conflict of the story is the problem the main character faces. Most stories have more than one conflict, but one is more important than the others.

Work with a small group to complete the chart below. In each novel, find a quotation that shows evidence of the type of conflict described in each row of the chart.

	Novel #1	Novel #2
Title		
Main Character		
Person vs. Person		
Quotation:		
Person vs. Self		
Quotation:		
Person vs. Society		
Quotation:		
Person vs. Nature		
Quotation:		

Discuss the following questions as a group. Record your answers on a separate piece of paper.

1. Which type of conflict is the most important for each main character?

2. What is similar about the two characters and the conflicts they face?

3. What is different about the two characters and the conflicts they face?

4. Were any of the conflict types not important for either character? Explain.

NAME(S): _____

GET SETTINGS, GO!

With a partner, list the different places that are described in each novel. Where does the action take place? Think about big settings (such as cities) and small settings (such as someone's bedroom). See how many different places you can name.

_____	_____
(Title of Novel #1)	*(Title of Novel #2)*

1. Which book do you think had more settings? _____

2. Why do you think the author needed to use more settings in this book?

_____

_____

_____

+ +

Practice Speaking and Listening: Answer each question aloud to your partner, and support your opinion with reasons. After listening to your partner's answer, paraphrase what he or she said and add any details that you believe your partner missed.

	Speaker 1	**Speaker 2**
Name		
	Question: Which location do you think is the most important in Novel #1? Why?	Paraphrase your partner's answer. Discuss any details you feel that he or she left out.
	Paraphrase your partner's answer. Discuss any details you feel that he or she left out.	**Question:** Which location do you think is the most important in Novel #2? Why?

NAME: _____

ON LOCATION

Imagine that one of the characters from one of the stories is transported through space and time and placed into the setting of the other novel. How would this character adapt? What challenges would he or she face?

Write a short scene or story that shows this character in his or her new surroundings. You can choose to include as many characters or other elements from the second story (or both if you wish). Have fun and be creative, but your scene or story must make sense for the character (from one story) and the setting (from the other).

_____

_____

_____

_____

_____

_____

_____

_____

_____

_____

_____

_____

_____

_____

_____

_____

_____

_____

_____

_____

_____

_____

_____

_____

_____

_____

_____

NAME: _____

THEME SEEDS

Many novels and stories written for a young audience contain similar themes and ideas. A theme is the message behind the whole story. A story or novel can have several themes.

+ +

Look at the "List of Common Themes." Choose a theme that appears in both stories.

Theme: _____

Title of Novel/Story: _____

1. In this story, what happens to show this theme? _____

_____

_____

    Give one quotation that supports your answer. _____

_____

_____ Page number(s): _____

Title of Other Novel/Story: _____

2. In this story, what happens to show this theme? _____

_____

_____

    Give one quotation that supports your answer. _____

_____

_____ Page number(s): _____

3. What is similar about the way this theme is used in both stories? Provide at least two details in your answer.

_____

_____

_____

4. What is different about the way this theme is used in both stories? Provide at least two details in your answer.

_____

_____

_____

SECTION LOG-IN

Use the prompts below to make a more personal connection to what you have read. Choose one of the following suggestions and use it to fill a page in your Interactive Novel Log. Take this opportunity to connect to the novel in a way that interests you.

Begin by reading each idea. Put a checkmark beside the ones that most appeal to you.

+ +

Ideas for Your Interactive Novel Log

☐ **In the Beginning** — Which of the two stories grabbed you the most in the beginning? Which one captured your imagination or had your attention right from the start? Why? Compare and contrast the way each story began. In your opinion, which one was more effective or exciting?

☐ **And In the End** — Which of the two stories had the most satisfying ending? Did either ending leave you wanting to know more? Explain.

☐ **He Said, She Said** — Imagine if a character from one of the stories could write an e-mail or letter to a character from the other story. What would he or she say? What advice would he or she give? Why would this character feel the need to reach out to the other character? Use the voice of your chosen character to write an e-mail or letter that answers these questions.

☐ **The Meet-Up** — Imagine that some of the characters from one story and some of the characters from the other are all in the same scene with each other. How would they interact? What would they say or do? Come up with a situation in which to put the characters. Decide the situation and the details that led to these characters being together in one place. Write a scene, either in paragraph form or in script form. What happens? How does it end?

☐ **Time Capsule** — A time capsule is a container that people fill with items that are meaningful to them at that time. It is then locked away or buried for people to find much later. Imagine that one of the characters in one of the stories created a time capsule. What would he or she put into it? Now imagine that a character from the other story found this time capsule. What would this character think about the other character's time capsule? What guesses might this character make about the other character? Why?

☐ **Other** — Come up with an idea of your own! Your idea should be related to the concept of comparing and/or contrasting the two pieces of literature you have just read.

_____

_____

GLOSSARY OF LITERARY TERMS

Most people learn to use specialized tools to perform tasks at the highest level. Authors are no different. Authors have a full set of tools that allow them to create literature that is interesting and full of depth.

Term	Explanation
cliffhanger	a device — often used at the end of chapters — in which a story builds a lot of tension but then ends abruptly without resolving the tension
climax	the most tense or exciting part of the story and the turning point when we begin to see how a conflict might end
conflict	a problem in the story, against which a character (or characters) must struggle to overcome
dynamic character	a character that changes his or her personality, opinions, or actions at some point or at several points in the story (A character who does not change is called a **static character**.)
flashback	a device used to show something that happened prior to the current action
foreshadowing	a warning or indication of an event that will happen in the future
genre	the category in which a novel fits based on the setting, conflicts, and characters contained within it
inference	a device in which the author does not directly state something in the text but allows the readers to use clues in the text, along with their own knowledge, to understand meaning
irony	a device in which the author leads the reader to expect one thing but then delivers the opposite
mood	the feeling of a scene, which could be shown in the atmosphere of a setting, the feelings of a character, etc.
pacing	the rhythm and flow of the text and/or the plot, which can be affected by such choices as word length, sentence length, and chapter length
personification	a device in which an author uses human attributes to describe something that is not human
plot	what happens in the story
point of view	who is telling the story (In **first-person**, the narrator is a character in the story. In **third-person**, the narrator is not a character in the story.)
protagonist	the main character in the novel (The person or force that opposes the protagonist is called the **antagonist**.)
resolution	the ending of a conflict
structure	the way the story is ordered and organized; the way events build on one another
symbolism	the use of a person, object, or idea to stand for or represent another person, object, or idea
theme	a message or big idea behind what happens in the story
tone	the author's attitude towards the characters, settings, events, etc., of the story
transition	the place in a piece of writing where one idea or storyline ends and another begins

LIST OF FICTION GENRES

A fiction novel can be about literally anything! There are no limits or boundaries to what can happen and what type of characters can exist in a work of fiction. However, certain character types and plots have appeared over and over again throughout the course of literature. It is based on the similarities between many works of fiction that we are able to put literature into categories, or genres. Here are some of the most common genres you will find. Some novels will only fit into one genre, while others contain elements of multiple genres.

Name of Genre	Elements Common to this Genre
Adventure	involves exciting or unusual experiences and events; danger-filled
Contemporary Fiction	features recognizable character types and technology/culture from our current time period
Drama	contains dialogue and stage directions and is intended to be performed
Fable	short story that includes a moral message and often features animal characters
Fairy Tale	usually written for children; can contain fairies and other magical creatures
Fantasy	fanciful, imaginative, and filled with unnatural events and characters
Graphic Novel	contains very few words; storyline formed from powerful images
Historical Novel	based on past events and often includes real historical figures interacting with fictional characters
Magical Realism	mostly resembles real life and real circumstances but contains a few magical or fantastical elements that are not possible in our world
Mythology	stories featuring ancient characters and intended to explain elements of nature, history, or customs
Realistic Fiction	meant to resemble real life and show people and events as they really are or have been
Science Fiction	takes place in the future when new technology exists and drives the action
Suspense/Thriller	exciting, action-filled story that often includes mysteries and/or cliffhangers
Young Adult Fiction	often deals with themes of growing up, gaining strength or wisdom, and finding acceptance
Western	usually set in the Wild West or other time when lawlessness ruled and great courage was needed

MEETING STANDARDS

The lessons and activities included in *Rigorous Reading: An In-Depth Guide for Any Novel* meet the following Common Core State Standards for grades 6–8. (©Copyright 2010. National Governors Association Center for Best Practices and Council of Chief State School Officers. All rights reserved.)

The code for each standard covered in this resource is listed in the table below and on pages 143–144. The codes are listed in boldface, and the page numbers of the activities that meet that standard are listed in regular type. For more information about the Common Core State Standards and for a full listing of the descriptions associated with each code, go to *http://www.corestandards.org/* or visit *http://www.teachercreated.com/standards/*.

Here is an example of an English Language Arts (ELA) code and how to read it:

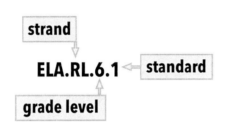

ELA Strands

L = Language
W = Writing
RL = Reading: Literature
SL = Speaking and Listening

+ +

College and Career Readiness Anchor Standards for Reading

ELA-Literacy.CCRA.R.1: 18–34, 38–46, 49–57, 60–68, 73, 75–79, 83–97, 99, 108–109, 111, 115–117, 120–123, 128–136, 138

ELA-Literacy.CCRA.R.2: 22–28, 31–33, 38–46, 49–50, 53–57, 62–68, 73–79, 83–88, 90–97, 99, 103–105, 108–109, 111, 113, 115–119, 122–123, 128–136, 138

ELA-Literacy.CCRA.R.3: 18–34, 39–40, 42–47, 49–51, 53–57, 61, 64–65, 67, 73, 75–77, 79, 83–85, 87–89, 91–93, 96–97, 108–109, 111, 114–115, 117, 122–123, 128–136, 138

ELA-Literacy.CCRA.R.4: 18–34, 38–57, 60–68, 70, 73–77, 79, 83–100, 102–105, 108–109, 111, 113, 115–117, 128–136, 138

ELA-Literacy.CCRA.R.5: 39–41, 44–47, 49–51, 53, 64, 66–68, 73, 75–79, 83–88, 91–92, 94, 96–97, 108–109, 111, 113, 115–117, 132–133

ELA-Literacy.CCRA.R.6: 28–34, 40, 43–45, 62–68, 73, 75–79, 83–93, 96–97, 113, 116–117, 130–131, 134–135

ELA-Literacy.CCRA.R.7: 14, 48–50, 54–57, 109, 111, 113–115, 120

ELA-Literacy.CCRA.R.9: 57, 79, 120, 128–139

ELA-Literacy.CCRA.R.10: 18–34, 38–57, 60–70, 73–79, 83–100, 102–105, 108–126, 128–139

College and Career Readiness Anchor Standards for Writing

ELA-Literacy.CCRA.W.1: 12–14, 18–28, 31–34, 39–43, 45–47, 51–54, 57, 61, 63–68, 73, 75–79, 83–85, 87, 90–92, 96–97, 108–109, 116–121, 128–136, 138–139

ELA-Literacy.CCRA.W.2: 11–14, 18–29, 31–34, 38–57, 60–68, 73, 75–79, 83–92, 94–97, 99–100, 103–105, 108–109, 111, 116–121, 128–136, 138–139

ELA-Literacy.CCRA.W.3: 30, 69–70, 79, 84, 100, 137, 139

ELA-Literacy.CCRA.W.4: 11–14, 18–34, 38–57, 60–70, 73–79, 83–92, 94–97, 99–100, 102–105, 108–109, 111, 116–121, 128–136, 138–139

ELA-Literacy.CCRA.W.5: 14, 54–56, 108–112, 116–119

ELA-Literacy.CCRA.W.7: 14, 62–63, 67, 79, 99

ELA-Literacy.CCRA.W.8: 14, 79, 99, 110–113

ELA-Literacy.CCRA.W.9: 14, 18–34, 38–57, 60–70, 73–79, 83–100, 102–105, 110–113, 128–139

ELA-Literacy.CCRA.W.10: 11–14, 18–34, 38–57, 60–70, 73, 75–79, 83–92, 94–97, 99–100, 102–105, 108–111, 116–126, 128–139

+ +

College and Career Readiness Anchor Standards for Speaking and Listening

ELA-Literacy.CCRA.SL.1: 11, 26, 29–30, 41, 43, 54, 60, 63, 66, 77, 89–90, 93, 110, 112–115, 122–123, 130, 133, 135–136
ELA-Literacy.CCRA.SL.2: 11, 26, 29–30, 41, 43, 54, 60, 63, 66, 77, 89, 93, 112–115, 122–123, 130, 133, 135–136
ELA-Literacy.CCRA.SL.3: 29, 43, 54, 63, 77, 89, 93, 110, 112–115, 136
ELA-Literacy.CCRA.SL.4: 26, 29–30, 43, 54, 60, 63, 77, 89, 93, 110, 112–115, 122–123, 130, 136
ELA-Literacy.CCRA.SL.5: 54–56, 112–115, 122–123
ELA-Literacy.CCRA.SL.6: 11, 26, 29–30, 41, 43, 54, 60, 63, 66, 77, 89–90, 93, 110, 112–115, 122–123, 130, 133, 135–136

College and Career Readiness Anchor Standards for Language

ELA-Literacy.CCRA.L.1: 11–14, 18–34, 38–57, 60–70, 73–79, 83–100, 102–105, 108–126, 128–139
ELA-Literacy.CCRA.L.2: 11–14, 18–34, 38–57, 60–70, 73–79, 83–100, 102–105, 108–114, 116–126, 128–139
ELA-Literacy.CCRA.L.3: 11–14, 18–34, 38–57, 60–70, 73–79, 83–100, 102–105, 108–126, 128–139
ELA-Literacy.CCRA.L.4: 14, 18–34, 38–57, 60–70, 73–79, 83–100, 102–105, 108–114, 116–126, 128–139
ELA-Literacy.CCRA.L.5: 18–34, 38–57, 60–70, 73–79, 83–100, 102–105, 108–126, 128–139
ELA-Literacy.CCRA.L.6: 11–14, 18–34, 38–57, 60–70, 73–79, 83–100, 102–105, 108–126, 128–139

+ +

Strand Reading: Literature   **Substrand** Key Ideas and Details

ELA.RL.6.1, ELA.RL.7.1, ELA.RL.8.1: 18–34, 39–46, 49–57, 60–68, 73, 75–79, 83–97, 99, 108–109, 111, 115–117, 120–123, 128–136, 138
ELA.RL.6.2, ELA.RL.7.2, ELA.RL.8.2: 29, 31–32, 38–46, 49–51, 53–55, 62–68, 73–79, 83–88, 90–97, 99, 103–105, 108–109, 111, 113, 115–119, 122–123, 128–136, 138
ELA.RL.6.3: 18–22, 38–46, 49–51, 53, 57, 64, 67, 73, 76–77, 83, 85–87, 92–93, 96–97, 108–109, 115–117, 128–133, 135, 138
ELA.RL.7.3: 18–33, 38–41, 49–51, 53, 60-68, 73, 75–79, 83, 86–97, 99, 112–113, 115–117, 128–138
ELA.RL.8.3: 18–27, 38–41, 49–51, 53, 57, 64–68, 73, 77, 79, 85–87, 91–97, 112–113, 115–117, 122–123, 128–131, 133–135, 138

Strand Reading: Literature   **Substrand** Craft and Structure

ELA.RL.6.4, ELA.RL.7.4, ELA.RL.8.4: 18–33, 38–57, 60–70, 73–79, 83–100, 102–105, 108–109, 111, 113, 115–117, 128–136, 138
ELA.RL.6.5: 22–24, 26, 31–32, 38–41, 43–46, 50–53, 57, 60–67, 73, 75–77, 83, 85–89, 91–97, 99, 108–109, 112–113, 115–117, 124–125, 132–133, 135–136, 138–139
ELA.RL.7.5: 84
ELA.RL.8.5: 83, 132–133, 139
ELA.RL.6.6: 28–34, 41, 61, 91–93, 116–117, 128–131, 134–135
ELA.RL.7.6: 18–21, 23–34, 61, 91–93, 116–117, 128–131, 134–135
ELA.RL.8.6: 22, 29–34, 79, 94

Strand Reading: Literature   **Substrand** Integration of Knowledge and Ideas

ELA.RL.6.7, ELA.RL.7.7, ELA.RL.8.7: 120

Strand Reading: Literature   **Substrand** Range of Reading and Level of Text Complexity

ELA.RL.6.10, ELA.RL.7.10, ELA.RL.8.10: 18–34, 38–57, 60–70, 73–79, 83–100, 102–105, 108–126, 128–139

MEETING STANDARDS (cont.)

+ +

Strand Writing   **Substrand** Text Types and Purposes

ELA.W.6.1, ELA.W.7.1, ELA.W.8.1: 11–14, 18–28, 31–34, 39–43, 45–47, 51–54, 57, 61, 63–68, 73, 75–79, 83–85, 87, 90–92, 96–97, 108–109, 116–121, 128–136, 138–139

ELA.W.6.2, ELA.W.7.2, ELA.W.8.2: 11–14, 18–29, 31–34, 38–57, 60–68, 73, 75–79, 83–92, 94–97, 99–100, 103–105, 108–109, 111, 116–121, 128–136, 138–139

ELA.W.6.3, ELA.W.7.3, ELA.W.8.3: 30, 69–70, 79, 84, 100, 137, 139

Strand Writing   **Substrand** Production and Distribution of Writing

ELA.W.6.4, ELA.W.7.4, ELA.W.8.4: 11–14, 18–34, 38–57, 60–70, 73–79, 83–92, 94–97, 99–100, 102–105, 108–109, 111, 116–121, 128–136, 138–139

ELA.W.6.5, ELA.W.7.5, ELA.W.8.5: 54–56, 108–112, 116–119

Strand Writing   **Substrand** Research to Build and Present Knowledge

ELA.W.6.7, ELA.W.7.7, ELA.W.8.7: 14, 62–63, 67, 79, 99, 110–113

ELA.W.6.8, ELA.W.7.8, ELA.W.8.8: 14, 29, 79, 99, 110–113, 128–139

ELA.W.6.9, ELA.W.7.9, ELA.W.8.9: 11, 13–14, 18–34, 38–57, 60–70, 73, 75–79, 83–100, 102–105

Strand Writing   **Substrand** Range of Writing

ELA.W.6.10, ELA.W.7.10, ELA.W.8.10: 11–14, 18–34, 38–57, 60–70, 73, 75–79, 83–92, 94–97, 99–100, 102–105, 108–111, 116–126, 128–139

+ +

Strand Speaking and Listening   **Substrand** Comprehension and Collaboration

ELA.SL.6.1, ELA.SL.7.1, ELA.SL.8.1: 11, 26, 29–30, 41, 43, 54, 60, 63, 66, 77, 89–90, 93

ELA.SL.6.2, ELA.SL.7.2, ELA.SL.8.2: 11, 26, 29–30, 41, 43, 54, 60, 63, 66, 77, 89, 93

ELA.SL.6.3, ELA.SL.7.3, ELA.SL.8.3: 29, 43, 54, 63, 77, 89, 93

Strand Speaking and Listening   **Substrand** Presentation of Knowledge and Ideas

ELA.SL.6.4, ELA.SL.7.4, ELA.SL.8.4: 11, 26, 29, 43, 54, 60, 63, 77, 89, 93

ELA.SL.6.5, ELA.SL.7.5, ELA.SL.8.5: 54–56

ELA.SL.6.6, ELA.SL.7.6, ELA.SL.8.6: 11, 26, 29–30, 41, 43, 54, 60, 63, 66, 77, 89–90, 93

+ +

Strand Language   **Substrand** Conventions of Standard English

ELA.L.6.1, ELA.L.7.1, ELA.L.8.1: 11–14, 18–34, 38–57, 60–70, 73–79, 83–100, 102–105, 108–126, 128–139

ELA.L.6.2, ELA.L.7.2, ELA.L.8.2: 11–14, 18–34, 38–57, 60–70, 73–79, 83–100, 102–105, 108–114, 116–126, 128–139

Strand Language   **Substrand** Knowledge of Language

ELA.L.6.3, ELA.L.7.3, ELA.L.8.3: 11–14, 18–34, 38–57, 60–70, 73–79, 83–100, 102–105, 108–126, 128–139

Strand Language   **Substrand** Vocabulary Acquisition and Use

ELA.L.6.4, ELA.L.7.4, ELA.L.8.4: 18–34, 38–57, 60–70, 73–79, 83–100, 102–105, 108–114, 116–126, 128–139

ELA.L.6.5, ELA.L.7.5, ELA.L.8.5: 18–34, 38–57, 60–70, 73–79, 83–100, 102–105, 108–126, 128–139

ELA.L.6.6, ELA.L.7.6, ELA.L.8.6: 11–14, 18–34, 38–57, 60–70, 73–79, 83–100, 102–105, 108–126, 128–139